MEMPHIS

MARGARET LITTMAN

Contents

MEMPHIS

MEMPHIS

Take away its music, and Memphis would lose its soul. Memphis may owe its existence to the mighty Mississippi, but it is music that has defined this Southern metropolis. Memphis music started with the spirituals and work songs of poor Mississippi Delta cotton farmers who came to Memphis and created a new sound: the Memphis blues. The blues then spawned its own offspring: soul, R&B, country, and, of course, rock 'n' roll as sung by a poor truck driver from Tupelo, Mississippi, named Elvis Presley.

On any given night you can find juke joints where the music flows as freely as the booze, and sitting still is not an option. On Beale Street, music wafts from inside smoky bars out onto the street, inviting you to come inside for a spell. And on Sundays, the sounds of old-fashioned spirituals and new gospel music can be heard at churches throughout the city.

Memphis music is the backbeat of any visit to the city, but it certainly is not the only reason to come. For as rich as Memphis's history is, this is a city that does not live in its past. Since the 1990s, Memphis has gone through a rebirth, giving new life to the region as a tourist destination. An NBA franchise (the Grizzlies) arrived, the National Civil Rights Museum opened on the grounds of the historic Lorraine Motel, a fantastic AAA baseball field opened downtown, and Memphis made its mark with films such as *Hustle & Flow, Forty Shades of*

© ANDREA ZUCKER/MEMPHIS VISITORS BUREAU

HIGHLIGHTS

years the Lorraine Motel merely represented the tragic assassination of Martin Luther King Jr. Today, it tells the story of the African American struggle for civil rights, from before the Civil War to the present day (page 15).

◖ The Peabody Hotel Memphis: Even the ducks in the fountain get the red-carpet treatment at this landmark hotel. The lobby is a must-visit, even for those who are not hotel guests (page 16).

◖ Stax Museum of American Soul Music: Irresistible soul music is what made Stax famous in the 1960s, and it is what makes the Stax museum sweet today. Exhibits bring to life the work of Otis Redding, the Staple Singers, Isaac Hayes, and more (page 23).

◖ Graceland: The Elvis phenomenon is alive and well, even if the King himself is not. Presley's south Memphis mansion is a testament not only to the King's music, but also his fans (page 23).

◖ Elmwood Cemetery: Perhaps the most surprising attraction in Memphis, Elmwood is the final resting place of dozens of Memphis characters: madames, blues singers, mayors, and pioneers of all types (page 26).

◖ Beale Street: The street that gave birth to the Memphis blues celebrates its legacy every single night of the week (page 11).

◖ National Civil Rights Museum: For

◖ Barbecue: Tangy, juicy, and just a little sweet, Memphis barbecue at places like the **Cozy Corner** is the stuff of dreams (page 49).

Blue, and *Black Snake Moan.* In 2011, more than 10 million people visited Memphis.

While you're here, you can sustain yourself on the city's world-famous barbecue, its fried chicken and catfish, and its homemade plate lunches, not to mention nouveau Southern eats. Eating may not be why you come, but it will be why you stay.

Memphis is a city of the South. More than just the largest city in Tennessee, Memphis is a hub for the entire Mid-South, which stretches from West Tennessee all the way down into Mississippi

and Arkansas. As such, the city is a melting pot of cultural, musical, culinary, and economic influences from the entire Mississippi River delta.

PLANNING YOUR TIME

You can knock out Memphis's main attractions in a weekend, but it takes a bit longer to soak up the city's special mojo: the music, food, and laid-back attitude. In fact, if you want more than just a taste of Memphis's famous blues, its legendary barbecue, or its rich history, plan to stay at least a week.

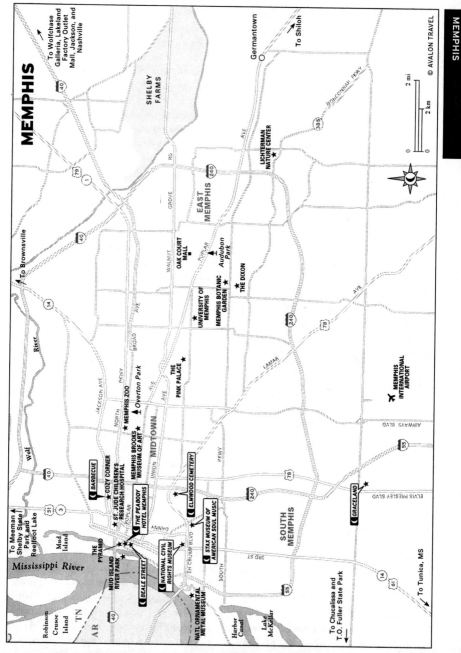

Choose downtown Memphis as your home base. The city center is home to the best bars, restaurants, sports venues, live music clubs, and, of course, Beale Street. Downtown is also the liveliest, and one of the safest, parts of Memphis after the sun sets.

While a lot of Memphis's attractions are downtown, others are located in the eastern and southern stretches of the city. A free shuttle is available to Graceland and Sun Studio from downtown, but for other attractions like the Stax Museum of American Soul Music and the Memphis Brooks Museum of Art, you will need a car or taxi. Take note that two of the city's best barbecue joints (a Memphis must), as well as its most famous juke joints, are not within walking distance of downtown.

When to Go

Memphis is a city with four seasons. The average temperature in January is 41°F, and in July it hits 81°F. Summer is certainly the most popular season for visiting—Elvis Week in August sees the most visitors of all—but the humid Memphis summer is not for the faint of heart.

The best time to visit Memphis is May, when summer is still fresh and mild, and the city puts on its annual Memphis in May celebration. Memphis in May includes the World Championship Barbeque Cooking Contest, the Beale Street Music Festival, and the Memphis International Festival.

Fall is also a good choice. The Memphis Music and Heritage Festival held over Labor Day weekend is a great reason to come to Memphis, and probably the best choice for fans of traditional Memphis music.

But if you can't come when the weather is temperate, don't fret. Memphis attractions are open year-round, and the city continues to rock, day in and day out.

ORIENTATION

Memphis is perched atop a low bluff overlooking the majestic Mississippi River (hence its nickname, Bluff City). The center city district lies, roughly speaking, along the river. Main Street, a pedestrian-only mall (except for the trolleys) runs north–south, while Union, Madison, and Poplar Avenues are the main east–west thoroughfares.

While not compact, central Memphis is entirely walkable for people willing to use a little shoe leather. The Main Street trolley makes it easy to see downtown and uptown attractions without a car.

In this guide, locations south of Union Avenue are considered **downtown,** while locations north are **uptown.** Downtown's main attraction is Beale Street. Also contained within the downtown district is the area known as **South Main,** a three-block strip along southern Main Street that is home to trendy boutiques, art galleries, restaurants, and condos. South Main is about a 15-minute walk or 5-minute trolley ride from Beale Street.

Another unique neighborhood in the city center is **The Pinch,** located along North Main Street past the I-40 overpass. Originally settled by German immigrants, the Pinch is now a hub of restaurants and nightlife. It is also the gateway to gentrifying residential neighborhoods farther north.

Restaurants in the Pinch have been categorized as uptown in this guide. You can walk to the Pinch, but the best way to get there is to ride the Main Street Trolley.

In 1989, developers created **Harbor Town,** a New Urban community on Mud Island. The concept was to create a city community that offered amenities such as schools, gyms, entertainment, and restaurants within walking distance of each other. It was also designed to promote a sense of community; homes were built close together with low fences, front porches, and small yards, so that residents would use community parks and green spaces.

In 2007, a boutique hotel opened in Harbor Town, putting the area on the accommodations map for the first time. A major draw for Harbor Town is that it is located right across the river from downtown Memphis but feels like a tight-knit residential community.

Memphis sprawls south, east, and north from the river. Head east from downtown, and you are in **midtown,** a district of strip malls, aging suburbs, and the city's best park and art museum. Poplar Avenue is the main artery of midtown, and it's a good point of reference when exploring by car (which is really the only way to get around midtown). The city's original suburb, midtown now seems positively urban compared to the sprawling burbs that creep farther eastward every year.

Located within midtown is **Cooper-Young,** a redeveloping residential and commercial neighborhood that lies around the intersection of Cooper Street and Young Avenue. Since the 1970s, residents of this neighborhood have fought the tide of urban decay by encouraging

investment, good schools, and amenities like parks, art galleries, and independent restaurants, and generally fostering a sense of pride in the area. The result is a neighborhood where you'll find lots of restaurants, a great used-book store, record shops, and other attractions that draw the city's young and young at heart.

East Memphis is where you will find large shopping malls, major hospitals, the University of Memphis, and lots of traffic jams. There are also a few attractions out here, the Dixon and the Memphis Botanic Gardens among them.

Generally speaking, **north and south Memphis** are the most economically depressed areas of the city. Visitors beat a path to attractions like Graceland and Stax in southern Memphis during the day but tend to avoid those areas at night, at least unless they are with a local who knows the way around.

Sights

DOWNTOWN
Downtown refers to the area south of Union Avenue in the city center. It is the heart of Memphis's tourist district.

◖ Beale Street
If you want to delve into the history and character of Memphis music, your starting point should be Beale Street, home of the blues.

A combination of forces led Beale Street to its place in musical history and popular culture. Named in the 1840s after a war hero, Beale Street was originally part of South Memphis, a separate city that rivaled Memphis during the 1840s.

Beginning in the 1850s, and continuing in greater numbers during and after the Civil War, African Americans began to settle along the western part of Beale Street. By the 1880s and 1890s, a middle class of black professionals began to emerge, and Beale Street became the center of commerce, entertainment, and life

for many of them. Together with black-owned businesses on Beale Street were laundries, bars, restaurants, pawn shops, and more operated by immigrants from eastern Europe, Ireland, China, Greece, and Germany.

From the 1880s until the 1960s, Beale Street was the epicenter of African American life, not just for Memphians but also for the entire Mid-South region. It was here that blacks felt free from many of society's restrictions.

Beale Street's decline began in the mid-20th century, and by the 1970s it was a shadow of its former self. Investment during the 1980s and '90s led to the street's rebirth as a destination for tourists and source of pride for residents, who could now show off the street that gave birth to the blues.

Today, Beale Street has two distinct personalities. During the day it is a laid-back place for families or adults to stroll, buy souvenirs, and eat. You can also stop at one of several museums and attractions located on the street. At night, Beale Street is a strip of nightclubs and restaurants, a great place to people-watch, and the best place in the state, if not the country, to catch live blues seven nights a week.

W. C. Handy Home and Museum

The story of Beale Street cannot be told without mentioning William Christopher Handy, whose Memphis home sits at the corner of Beale Street and 4th Avenue. The building was

originally located at 659 Jeanette Street, but it was moved to Beale Street in 1985. Now the W. C. Handy Home and Museum (352 Beale St., 901/527-3427, wchandymemphis.org, summer Tues.–Sat. 10 A.M.–5 P.M., winter Tues.–Sat. 11 A.M.–4 P.M., adults $4, children $3) is dedicated to telling the story of Handy's life. It was Handy who famously wrote, in his "Beale Street Blues": "If Beale Street could talk, married men would have to take their beds and walk, except one or two who never drink booze, and the blind

BEALE STREET WALKING TOUR

Beale Street runs from the Mississippi River to Manassas Street in midtown Memphis, but it is the three blocks between 2nd and 4th Streets that really matter. In its heyday, the Beale Street commercial and entertainment district extended farther east and west, but today, it has been condensed into the half dozen blocks from Main Street to 4th Street. This walking tour begins at the intersection of Beale and Main Streets, and heads eastward.

Near the corner of Beale and Main Streets is the **Orpheum Theatre** (203 S. Main St., 901/525-7800, www.orpheum-memphis.com). This site has been used for entertainment since 1890, when the Grand Opera House opened there with a production of *Les Huguenots*. Later, the opera house presented vaudeville shows and theater. Fire destroyed it in 1923, but in 1928 it reopened as the Orpheum, a movie theater and performing arts venue for the likes of Duke Ellington, Cab Calloway, Bob Hope, and Mae West. The Orpheum remains one of the city's premier venues for the performing arts, with Broadway productions, mainstream musical artists, and movies.

A block east of the Orpheum is a statue of Memphis's most famous native son, Elvis Presley. Depicting the King during his early career, the statue sits in **Elvis Presley Plaza.**

A. Schwab (163 Beale St., 901/523-9782, Mon.-Fri. 9 A.M.-5 P.M.) has served Memphis residents for more than 130 years, although it focuses now on odd, out-of-date, and hard-to-find items rather than general store necessities. Stop in for a souvenir or to visit the A. Schwab "museum," a collection of old-fashioned household tools and implements.

A few doors down from A. Schwab, at the Irish pub Silky O'Sullivan's, you can see what remains of one of Beale Street's most magnificent old buildings. The facade of what was once the **Gallina Building** is held up by six steel girders. From the 1860s until 1914, this facade kept watch on the business empire of Squire Charles Gallina, who operated a saloon, restaurant, and 20-room hotel, as well as a gambling room.

Beyond 3rd Street is **Handy Park,** named for famous blues composer and musician W.C. Handy. Beale Street's market house was torn down in 1930 to build the park. Since it opened,

Handy Park has been a popular place for street musicians, peddlers, concerts, and community events, all of which are presided over by the life-size statue of W.C. Handy.

About midway up the southern side of the next block of Beale Street is the **Daisy Theater** (329 Beale St.), built in 1917 as a movie house. Much of the original interior remains today. The theater is closed to the public but may be rented for private events. Contact the Beale Street Development Corporation (866/406-5986) for information.

Across the street from the Daisy Theater is the **New Daisy Theater,** built in 1941 as another movie house. The New Daisy is one of Memphis's prime live music venues, and it books rock and alternative acts from around the country.

Stately and old, the **First Baptist Beale Street Church** (379 Beale St.) was built between 1868 and 1885 and is home to one of the oldest African American congregations in Memphis. In the 1860s, the congregation started to meet under brush arbors at the present location, and the first temporary structure was erected in 1865. The cornerstone was laid for the present building in 1871. The First Baptist Beale Street Church was an important force in Memphis's African American history. It was here that black Memphians published their first newspapers, the *Memphis Watchman* and the *Memphis Free Speech and Headlight.*

Today, **Church Park** is a relatively nondescript city park with benches and some paved walks. But in 1899, when Robert Church built Church Park and Auditorium at the eastern end of the Beale Street commercial district, the park was something truly special. Church, the mixed-race son of a white steamboat captain, is said to have been the first black millionaire in the South. He was troubled that there were no public parks expressly for Memphis's African American residents, so in 1899 he opened Church Park and Auditorium on six acres of land along Beale Street. The park was beautifully landscaped and manicured, with bright flowers, tropical trees, and peacocks. The auditorium was a venue for black performers and speakers. Church Park remains a venue for community events, particularly the annual Africa in April event every spring.

man on the corner singing 'Beale Street Blues.' I'd rather be there than anyplace I know."

The Handy museum houses photographs of Handy's family, one of his band uniforms, and memorabilia of the recording company that he founded. You can also hear samples of Handy's music.

A. Schwab

During Beale Street's dark days of the 1970s and '80s, when the clubs and restaurants closed and the pawn shops opened, one mainstay remained: A. Schwab (163 Beale St., 901/523-9782, Mon.–Wed. 10 A.M.–8 P.M., Thurs.–Sat. 10 A.M.–10 P.M., Sun. noon–8 P.M.). This landmark general store opened in 1876 and was owned and operated by the same family until 2011. Originally the source for household necessities for thousands of Delta residents, A. Schwab remains a treasure trove of goods. Here

W. C. HANDY

W. C. Handy was born in a log cabin in Florence, Alabama, in 1873. The son and grandson of African Methodist Episcopal ministers, Handy was exposed to music as a child in his father's church. Handy was also drawn to the music of the black laborers of the area, and when he moved to Memphis in the early 20th century, he recognized the wealth of the blues music he heard in bars, on street corners, and in back alleys around Beale Street.

Handy was a trained musician, so he was able to set down on paper the music that had, up until then, been passed from one musician to another.

In 1909 Handy composed Memphis mayor Ed Crump's campaign song, "Mr. Crump," which he later published as the "Memphis Blues." But he is most famous for his composition "St. Louis Blues," published in 1914. Handy also created the "Yellow Dog Blues," "Joe Turner Blues," and "Beale Street Blues." Known as the Father of the Blues, Handy passed away in 1958.

you will find practical things like underwear, hats, umbrellas, cookware, and tools, as well as novelties like old-fashioned candy, incense, and actual cans of Tennessee whoop-ass. Upstairs is the A. Schwab museum, a hodgepodge of old-time tools, clothes, and memorabilia of the store's 130-plus-year history.

The new owners, who purchased the store from the Schwab family in late 2011, plan to restore the exterior facade, expand the eclectic inventory, improve the second-floor museum, and add a soda fountain.

Memphis Rock 'n' Soul Museum

Music fans should plan to spend several hours at the Memphis Rock 'n' Soul Museum (191 Beale St., 901/205-2533, www.memphis-rocknsoul.org, daily 10 A.M.–7 P.M., adults $11, children 5–17 $8), located right next to FedEx Forum off Beale Street. An affiliate of the Smithsonian Institution, this museum tells the story of Memphis music from the Delta blues to *Shaft*. Start with a short video documentary, and then follow the exhibits with your personal audio guide, which includes recordings of dozens of Memphis-influenced artists from B. B. King to Elvis. Exhibits are dedicated to Memphis radio stations; the influence of the Victrola, Sam Phillips, and Sun Studio; and, of course, all things Elvis, among others. It takes several hours to study all the exhibits in detail and to listen to all (or even most) of the music, so plan accordingly.

There is a free shuttle that runs between the Rock 'n' Soul Museum, Graceland, and Sun Studio. Look for the black van with the Sun label's distinctive yellow sun on the side.

Gibson Guitar Factory

Across the street from the Rock 'n' Soul Museum is the Gibson Guitar Factory (145 Lt. George Lee Ave., 901/544-7998, ext. 4075, www.gibson.com, tours Mon.–Sat. every hour on the hour 11 A.M.–4 P.M., Sun. noon–4 P.M.,

© WAYNE HSIEH

The Lorraine Motel, where Dr. Martin Luther King Jr. was assassinated, now houses the National Civil Rights Museum.

org, Mon. and Wed.–Sat. 9 A.M.–5 P.M., Sun. 1–5 P.M., adults $13, students and seniors $11, children 4–17 $9.50). Built on the Lorraine Motel site where Dr. Martin Luther King Jr. was assassinated on April 4, 1968, the museum makes a thorough examination of the American civil rights movement from slavery to the present day. Exhibits display original letters, audio recordings, photos, and newspaper clippings from events including the Montgomery bus boycott, *Brown v. Board of Education,* Freedom Summer, and the march from Selma to Montgomery. Original and re-created artifacts, such as the bus where Rosa Parks made her stand in 1955 and the cell where Dr. King wrote his famous *Letter from a Birmingham Jail,* help to illustrate the story of civil rights.

When Dr. King visited Memphis in March and then again in April 1968, the Lorraine Motel was one of the handful of downtown hotels that welcomed African Americans. The room (and balcony and parking lot) where he spent his final hours has been carefully re-created, and narration by those who were with him tell the shocking story of his death. Across Mulberry Street, in the building that was once the boardinghouse from where James Earl Ray is believed to have fired his sniper shot, exhibits probe various theories about the assassination, as well as the worldwide legacy of the civil rights movement.

Visitors to the museum can pay an extra $2 for an audio guide—a worthwhile investment. You are asked not to take flash photography inside the museum. This is a large museum, and it is overflowing with information, so visitors who want to give the displays their due attention should plan on spending 3–4 hours here. A good way to visit would be to tour the Lorraine Motel exhibits first, take a break for lunch, and then go across the street for the second half of the museum when you are refreshed.

Spending half a day here is a powerful experience, and one that raises many thoughts

ages five and up $10), one of three in the United States. The Memphis plant specializes in the semi-hollow-bodied guitar, and a wide range of models are on sale in Gibson's retail shop. On the hour-long tour of the factory floor you can see guitars being made, from the shaping of the rim and panels to the painting and buffing of the finished product. Tours sell out, so reservations are recommended, particularly during the busier summer months. Most factory workers leave by 3 P.M. and have the weekends off, so plan ahead if you want to see the factory floor in full swing.

◖ National Civil Rights Museum

If you do nothing else while you are in Memphis, or, frankly, the state, visit the National Civil Rights Museum (450 Mulberry St., 901/521-9699, www.civilrightsmuseum.

about civil rights. Expect interesting conversations with your travel companions after coming here. The gift shop offers books and videos for more reading on the topic.

Admission is free on Monday after 3 P.M. to Tennessee residents. In June, July, and August the museum stays open until 6 P.M.

Belz Museum of Asian and Judaic Art

The Belz Museum of Asian and Judaic Art (119 S. Main St., 901/523-2787, www.belzmuseum. org, Tues.–Fri. 10 A.M.–5:30 P.M., Sat.–Sun. noon–5 P.M., adults $6, seniors $5, children $4), formerly Peabody Place Museum, houses one of the largest collections of artwork from the Q'ing dynasty. Forged from the private collection of Memphis developers Jack and Marilyn Belz, owners of the Peabody Hotel and the now shuttered Peabody Place mall, the museum features some 1,000 objects, including an array of jade, tapestries, paintings, furniture, carvings, and other artifacts. The museum is also home to the largest U.S. collection of work by Israeli artist Daniel Kafri.

UPTOWN

Uptown refers to locations along Union Avenue and points north in the center city district. Here downtown workers are more common than tourists, and tall office buildings rise above the city blocks.

The Cotton Museum

The Cotton Museum at the Memphis Cotton Exchange (65 Union Ave., 901/531-7826, www.memphiscottonmuseum.org, Mon.–Sat. 10 A.M.–5 P.M., Sun. noon–5 P.M., adults $10, seniors $9.50, students $9, children 6–12 $8) is located in the broad rectangular room that once was the nerve center of the Mid-South's cotton trade. The Cotton Exchange was established in 1873, and it was here that buyers and sellers of the South's most important cash crop

met, and where fortunes were made and lost. Located just steps away from the Mississippi River, the Exchange was the trading floor of Cotton Row, the area of town that was defined by the cotton industry.

The Cotton Museum is home to exhibits about cotton's history, its uses, and the culture that its cultivation gave rise to in Memphis and the Mississippi Delta. There are several videos you can watch, as well as a live Internet feed of today's cotton exchange—now conducted entirely electronically. The nicest thing about the museum, however, is seeing the chalkboard where the prices of cotton around the world were written by hand. There is also a replica of the Western Union office where buyers and sellers sent telegrams using an intricate system of abbreviations known only to the cotton trade. The museum expanded in 2010, with more hands-on exhibits and an educational wing.

◖ The Peabody Hotel Memphis

The Peabody Hotel Memphis (149 Union Ave., 901/529-4000, www.peabodymemphis.com) is the city's most famous hotel. Founded in 1869, the Peabody was one of the first grand hotels of the South, a place as well known for its elegant balls and big-band concerts as for the colorful characters who sipped cocktails at its famous lounge. Named in memory of the philanthropist George Peabody, the original hotel was located at the corner of Main and Monroe. It closed in 1923, and a new Peabody opened two years later in its present location on Union Avenue. It remained the place to see and be seen for generations of Memphians and Delta residents. It was David Cohn who famously wrote in 1935 that "the Mississippi Delta begins in the lobby of The Peabody Hotel."

Even if you don't stay here, you must stop by the elegant hotel lobby to see the twice-daily march of the Peabody ducks. They live on the roof of the hotel and make the journey—by elevator—to the lobby fountain every morning

© THE PEABODY MUSEUM/MEMPHIS VISITORS BUREAU

Ducks get the literal red-carpet treatment at the Peabody Hotel Memphis.

at 11 A.M. At 5 P.M. they march out of the fountain, back onto the elevator, and up to their accommodations on the roof.

The hotel employs a duck master who takes care of the ducks and supervises their daily trip downstairs. Watching the ducks is free, frenzied, and undeniably fun. It is also one of the most popular activities among visitors to Memphis, so be sure to get there early and secure a good vantage point along the red carpet to watch the duck march.

Mud Island

In Memphis, it is sometimes easy to forget that you are just steps away from the great Mississippi River. A trip to Mud Island will cure this misperception once and for all. A narrow band of land in the river, Mud Island is home to the **Mud Island River Park and Museum** (125 N. Front St., 901/576-7241, www.mudisland. com, Apr.–Oct. Tues.–Sun. 10 A.M.–5 P.M., adults $10, seniors $9, children $7), which has

exhibits about early uses of the river, steam- and paddleboats, floods, and much more.

The park's **Mississippi River Museum** begins with a refresher course on European exploration of this region—de Soto, La Salle, and Marquette and Joliet—followed by information about early settlement. The highlight is being able to explore a replica of a 1870s steamboat. In the Riverfolk Gallery there are wax depictions of Mark Twain, riverboat gambler George Devol, and steamship entertainers. The museum also remembers the numerous river disasters that have taken place along the Mississippi.

Admission to the museum includes the **River Walk** at the Mud Island River Park, a five-block scale model of the entire Mississippi River—from Minnesota to the Gulf of Mexico. Walk along the model to see scale representations of cities along the river's path, and read placards about the river's history. On a hot day, wear your bathing suit so you can swim in the pool at the end.

The river park is also home to an outdoor amphitheater, which in summer hosts big-name concerts, a snack bar, outdoor tables, and restrooms. You can rent canoes, kayaks, and pedal boats to use in the still waters around the Mud Island harbor. Bike rental is also available. Mud Island is the site of the annual Duncan–Williams Dragon Boat Races.

Admission to the river park is free. You cay pay $4 round-trip to ride the monorail to Mud Island, or you can walk across the monorail bridge for free. The monorail station is on Front Street at Adams Avenue.

Slavehaven Underground Railroad Museum

The legend of the Burkle Estate, a modest white clapboard house on North 2nd Street, has given rise to the Slavehaven Underground Railroad Museum (826 N. 2nd St., 901/527-3427, summer Mon.–Sat. 10 A.M.–4 P.M., winter Wed.–Sat. 10 A.M.–4 P.M., adults $6, youth $4). The museum here tells the story of slavery and the legendary Underground Railroad, which helped thousands of slaves escape to freedom in the North (and, after the 1850 Fugitive Slave Act, to Canada). Jacob Burkle, a German immigrant and owner of the Memphis stockyard, is said to have built the Burkle Estate around 1850. Escaping slaves would have hidden in a root cellar beneath the house before making the 1,500-foot trip to the banks of the Mississippi, where they made a further journey north.

Skeptics say that there is no evidence of this story and even point to documents that show that Burkle may not have purchased the property until 1871, well after the end of slavery. Advocates for the Underground Railroad story say that it was the nature of the railroad to be secret, so there is nothing unusual about a lack of concrete evidence.

The River Walk on Mud Island is a maze of fun.

THE BIRTH OF MUD ISLAND

Mud Island rose from the Mississippi River as a result of two seemingly small events. In 1876, the river shifted slightly about 20 miles south of Memphis, causing the currents that flowed past the city to alter course. And then, in 1910, the U.S. Navy gunboat *Amphitrite* anchored at the mouth of the Wolf River for almost two years, causing a further change in silt patterns. When the ship left in 1912, the sandbar continued to grow, and Mud Island was born.

Residents initially disliked the island, since it was ugly and proved to be a danger to river navigation.

Beginning in the 1930s, poor Memphians squatted on Mud Island in ramshackle homes built of scrap metal and wood. Between 200 and 500 people lived on the island during this time.

In 1959, a downtown airport was built on the island, but the airport was closed in 1970 when the DeSoto Bridge was built. In 1974, plans were developed for what is the present-day Mud Island River Park, which includes a full-scale replica of a riverboat, a monorail to the island, and the signature 2,000-foot flowing replica of the Mississippi River.

Visitors today need not be too concerned with the details of the debate; the Slavehaven museum does a good job of highlighting the brutality of the slave trade and slavery, and the ingenuity and bravery it took for slaves to escape. Perhaps the most interesting part of the exhibit are the quilts that demonstrate the way that slaves used quilting patterns to send messages to one another. Other displays show advertisements for Memphis slave auctions and images from the early 20th century that depict damaging racial stereotypes.

The museum is operated by Heritage Tours of Memphis, and staff are available to conduct guided tours of the property.

Fire Museum of Memphis

The Fire Museum of Memphis (118 Adams Ave., 901/320-5650, www.firemuseum.com, Mon.–Sat. 9 A.M.–5 P.M., adults $6, seniors $4, children $5) is a good place to take children. There is a huge display of fire-engine toys, lots of firefighting paraphernalia, and a "fire room" that presents important lessons on fire safety. You can also see old-fashioned fire engines, and youngsters will enjoy playing in the kid-friendly fire truck. The museum is located in the old Fire Station No. 1 in downtown Memphis. Admission is two-for-one on Tuesday.

St. Jude Children's Research Hospital

The sprawling complex of St. Jude Children's Research Hospital on uptown's northern fringe has been saving lives and bringing hope to children and their families since 1962. St. Jude was founded by entertainer Danny Thomas in fulfillment of his promise to God to give back to those in need. Over the years and thanks to the success of its fundraising arm—the American Lebanese Syrian Associated Charities—St. Jude has expanded many times over and now leads the world in research and treatment of catastrophic childhood diseases, especially pediatric cancers. The hospital never turns anyone away due to inability to pay, and it never makes families without insurance pay for their treatment.

Visitors can tour a small museum about Danny Thomas and St. Jude in the **Danny Thomas ALSAC Pavilion** (332 N. Lauderdale St., 901/495-4414, www.stjude.org, Sun.–Fri. 8:30 A.M.–4:30 P.M., Sat. 10 A.M.–4 P.M., free), located inside a golden dome on the hospital grounds. Just outside are the graves of Danny Thomas and his wife, Rose Marie.

The Pyramid

The Memphis Pyramid is the most physically dominating feature of the northern city skyline. Memphis's affiliation with all things Egypt began with its name and continued in 1897,

© WAYNE HSIEH

Memphis's Pyramid may be in flux, but it is still an icon on the skyline.

when a large-scale replica of a pyramid was built to represent Memphis at the Tennessee Centennial Exhibition in Nashville. Pyramids were popular symbols on Memphis paraphernalia for many years.

The first serious proposal for a life-size pyramid to be built in Memphis was written in the 1970s, but the idea did not take off until the 1980s, when the city and county governments agreed to fund it. Denver developer Sidney Shlenker promoted the plan and promised restaurants, tourist attractions, and lots of revenue for the city. The 321-foot pyramid was built and opened in 1991, minus the money-making engines that Shlenker promised. Today, the $63 million "Great American Pyramid" sits empty. Plans are in the works to turn the former Pyramid Arena into a retail center by August 2013.

MIDTOWN

You'll need a car to explore the attractions in midtown, which sprawls along Union, Poplar,

and Madison Avenues as they head eastward from the city center.

Sun Studio

It is well worth your time to drop by the famous Sun Studio (706 Union Ave., 800/441-6249, www.sunstudio.com, daily 10 A.M.–6 P.M., $12), where Elvis Presley recorded his first hit, "That's All Right," and where dozens of blues, rock, and country musicians were recorded during the 1950s. Founded by radio man and audio engineer Sam Phillips and his wife, Becky, the studio recorded weddings, funerals, events, and, of course, music. Phillips was interested in the blues, and his first recordings were of yet-unknown artists such as Rufus Thomas and Howlin' Wolf. In 1953, Elvis Presley came into the studio on his lunch break to record a $3 record of himself singing "My Happiness" for his mother. Phillips was not impressed with the performance, and it was not for another year—and thanks to the prodding of Phillips's

Lauderdale Courts

The least-known Elvis attraction in Memphis is Lauderdale Courts (252 N. Lauderdale St., 901/523-8662, www.lauderdalecourts.com), the public housing complex where Presley lived with his parents from 1949 to 1953 before his rise to fame. The handsome brick building was saved from the wrecking ball in the 1990s thanks to its history with the King, and the apartment where the Presleys lived has been restored to its 1950s glory. Most of the year, the Lauderdale Courts Elvis suite is rented out as a hotel room, but during Elvis's Birthday Week in January and Elvis Week in August it is open for public tours.

Victorian Village

Set on a tree-lined block of Adams Avenue near Orleans Street is Victorian Village, where a half dozen elegant Victorian-era homes escaped the "urban renewal" fate of other historic Memphis homes.

Visitors can tour the **Woodruff-Fontaine House** (680 Adams Ave., 901/526-1469, www.woodruff-fontaine.com, Wed.–Sun. noon–4 P.M., adults $10), one of the street's most magnificent buildings. Built starting in 1870 for the Woodruff family and sold to the Fontaines in the 1880s, the house was occupied through 1930, when it became part of the James Lee Art Academy, a precursor to the Memphis Academy of Art. When the academy moved in 1959, the building became city property and stood vacant. Beginning in 1961, city residents raised funds to restore and refurnish the house with period furniture and accessories, and it opened as a museum in 1964. This was during the period of urban renewal that saw to the demolition of many of Memphis's other old homes, and some of the house's furnishings were taken from homes that were later demolished. Visitors to the house are given a guided tour of the 1st floor and can explore the 2nd and 3rd floors on their own. This is a good stop if you are interested in antiques.

© WAYNE HSIEH

Sam Phillips made music history from the Sun Studio front office.

assistant, Marion Keisker—that Phillips called Presley in to record some more. When Phillips heard Elvis's version of the blues tune "That's All Right," he knew he had a hit. And he did.

But the story of Elvis's discovery is just one of many that took place in the modest homemade Sun Studio, and this attraction is not just for Elvis fans. The one-hour tour of the studio leaves every hour on the half hour, and while you are waiting you can order a real fountain drink from the snack bar or browse the shop's collection of recordings and paraphernalia. The studio is still in business; you can record here for $75 an hour at night, and dozens of top-notch performers have, including Grace Potter, Beck, and Matchbox 20.

Tours start every half hour during business hours and take approximately 90 minutes. Children under the age of five are not permitted on the tours. There are free shuttles from Graceland and the Rock 'n' Soul Museum to Sun Studio.

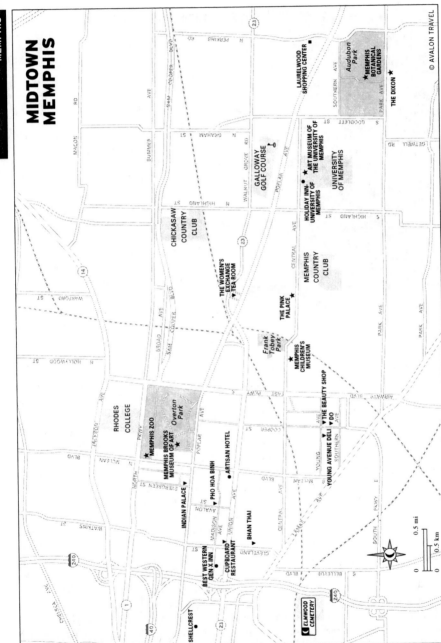

MIDTOWN
MEMPHIS

© AVALON TRAVEL

The **Magevney House** (198 Adams Ave., 901/526-1484) and the **Mallory-Neely House** (652 Adams Ave., 901/523-1484) are two other historical homes in the district. The Magevney House is the oldest middle-class residence still standing in Memphis. It was built in 1836 by an Irish immigrant to the city, Eugene Magevney. The Mallory-Neely House is of the same vintage and is notable for the fact that it was not refurnished in more than 100 years and so remains remarkably true to the era in which it was built.

The Magevney and Mallory-Neely Houses are owned by the City of Memphis, and due to budget cuts the interiors have been closed to the public. Call to find out if they have been reopened or just walk by to see the exteriors.

Memphis Brooks Museum of Art

Memphis's foremost art museum is located in Overton Park in midtown, a short drive from downtown. Memphis Brooks Museum of Art (1934 Poplar Ave., 901/544-6200, www.brooks-museum.org, Wed. and Fri. 10 A.M.–4 P.M., Thurs. 10 A.M.–8 P.M., Sat. 10 A.M.–5 P.M., Sun. 11 A.M.–5 P.M., adults $7, seniors $6, students $3) is the largest fine-art museum in Tennessee, and its permanent collection includes 8,000 works of art. This includes ancient African and Asian art, as well as European, American, and contemporary art. There are 29 galleries at the Brooks, and special exhibitions have focused on the work of Annie Leibovitz, men's fashion in Africa, and the silver work of Paul de Lamerie. There is also a museum shop and restaurant, as well as an auditorium often used to screen films.

The Memphis Zoo

The Memphis Zoo (2000 Prentiss Pl., 901/333-6500, www.memphiszoo.org, Mar.–Oct. daily 9 A.M.–5 P.M., Nov.–Feb. daily 9 A.M.–4 P.M., adults $15, children $10) has been expanding and is now the proud steward of two giant pandas, Le Le and Ya Ya; large cats; penguins; lions; tropical birds; and 3,500 other animal species. More hippos have been born here than at any other zoo. Its butterfly exhibit, open May–October, is a popular favorite, and camel rides are available in the spring. The zoo is located on the grounds of Overton Park. Parking is an additional $5.

SOUTH MEMPHIS
◖ Stax Museum of American Soul Music

There is no place in Memphis that better tells the story of the city's legendary soul music than the Stax Museum of American Soul Music (926 E. McLemore Ave., 901/946-7685, www.stax-museum.com, Tues.–Sat. 10 A.M.–5 P.M. and Sun. 1–5 P.M., additionally, Apr.–Oct. Mon. 1–5 P.M., adults $12, seniors, students, and military $11, children 9–12 $9).

The museum tour starts with a short toe-tapping video that sets the scene for the musical magic that took place here during the 1960s. Exhibits include the sanctuary of an old clapboard Delta church, which illustrates the connection between soul and gospel music. You can also see Booker T. Jones's original organ, Otis Redding's favorite suede leather jacket, and Isaac Hayes's 1972 peacock-blue gold-trimmed Cadillac Eldorado, Superfly.

The museum also takes you through the studio's control room and into the studio itself, slanted floors and all. If you want to try your hand, there is a karaoke machine, and a dance floor in case you can't help but move to the music. The Stax museum is a must-see for music enthusiasts but also an educational journey for those who don't know the story behind some of America's most famous songs. It sits next door to the Stax Music Academy, a present-day music school that reaches out to neighborhood youth.

◖ Graceland

Drive south from downtown on Elvis Presley Boulevard to reach the King's most famous

SOULSVILLE

A lucky convergence of people, talents, and social forces led to one of Memphis's – and America's – most distinctive musical stories. Stax Records was founded in 1960 by Jim Stewart, an aspiring country fiddler, and his sister, Estelle Axton. The first two letters of the brother and sister's surnames came together to form Stax, a name now synonymous with the raw Memphis sound of performers like Rufus and Carla Thomas, Otis Redding, Sam and Dave, Isaac Hayes, Eddie Floyd, the Mar-Keys, the Staple Singers, and Booker T. & the MGs.

Jim Stewart chose a closed movie theater in a working-class South Memphis neighborhood for his recording studio. He was on a tight budget, so he didn't bother to fix the sloped theater floor or angled walls, and the room's reverberating acoustics came to define the Memphis sound.

Motown was known as "Hitsville" for its smooth and palatable sound, so the artists at Stax began to call their neighborhood "Soulsville," a name that still refers to the area of South Memphis where Stax is located. The soul music that Stax recorded was raw and inventive, influenced by country, blues, gospel, and jazz.

The label's first hit was with WDIA-AM disc jockey Rufus Thomas and his daughter, Carla Thomas, who came in one day and recorded "Cause I Love You." The song became an overnight sensation.

Stax tapped into the talent of the neighborhood, and particularly the African American Booker T. Washington High School, which graduated such greats as the members of the Soul Children and the Mad Lads. As the Stax reputation developed, artists came from out of town to record, including a 21-year-old Otis Redding, who drove up from Georgia in hopes of making a record and made a career instead.

Stax also operated Satellite Records right next door to the studio, and here Estelle Axton was able to quickly test-market new recordings on the neighborhood youngsters who came in for the latest music. Wayne Jackson, a member of the studio's house band, the Memphis Horns, recalls that Estelle and Jim would invite hundreds of young people from the neighborhood into the studio to listen to their newest recording. Based on the group's response, they would choose the single.

Stax was unique for its time as an integrated organization, where the love of music trumped racial differences. As the civil rights movement evolved, Stax artists turned to serious social themes in their music. In 1972 Stax artists organized WattStax, an outdoor black music festival in Los Angeles.

Between 1960 and 1975, when the Stax magic ran out, the studio produced 800 singles and 300 albums, including 243 Top 100 and 14 number-one R&B hits. Isaac Hayes's theme from the movie *Shaft* was the fastest-selling album in Stax history, and one of three Stax songs went to number one on the pop charts. Other big Stax hits were Otis Redding's "(Sittin' on) The Dock of the Bay," the Staples Singers' "Respect Yourself," and Sam and Dave's "Soul Man."

Sadly, Stax was destroyed financially by a bad distribution deal with CBS Records in 1975, and the studio was closed. Its rare master tapes were sold at auction, and the studio where soul was born was demolished.

Thankfully, the story of Stax has not been forgotten. In 2001 ground was broken for a new Stax story, one that grew into the present-day music academy and the Stax Museum of American Soul Music.

home, Graceland (3717 Elvis Presley Blvd., 901/332-3322 or 800/238-2000, www.elvis.com, Mar.–Oct. Mon.–Sat. 9 A.M.–5 P.M., Sun. 10 A.M.–4 P.M., Nov. daily 10 A.M.–4 P.M., Dec.–Feb. Wed.–Mon. 10 A.M.–4 P.M., adults $32, seniors and students $28.80, children 7–12 $14, children 6 and under free). There is plenty of parking.

Visitors can choose from three tour packages: The mansion-only tour takes about an hour and costs $32; the platinum tour includes the automobile museum, Elvis's two airplanes, and other special perks for $36. Enthusiasts can choose the VIP package for $70, which gives you "front of the line" access, an all-day pass, keepsakes, and access to exclusive exhibits, such as one that features Elvis's first-ever professional photographs, taken in 1955.

The Graceland complex blends into the strip malls and fast-food joints that line the boulevard in this part of Memphis. The ticket counter, shops, and restaurants are located on the west side of the boulevard, and here you board a shuttle van that drives across the highway and up the curved drive to the Graceland mansion. Graceland managers may have taken full advantage of the commercial opportunities presented by the home that Elvis left behind, but they have not overdone it. The operation is laid-back, leaving the spotlight on Elvis and, of course, his fans, who travel to Memphis from around the world to visit.

The mansion tour is conducted by audio guide. It includes the ground floor of the mansion (the upstairs remains closed to the public) and several outbuildings that now house exhibits about Elvis's life and career.

High points include watching the press conference Elvis gave after leaving the army, witnessing firsthand his audacious taste in decor, and visiting the meditation garden where Elvis, his parents, and his grandmother are buried. There is also a plaque in memory of Elvis's lost twin, Jesse Garon. The audio tour plays many of Elvis's songs, family stories remembered by Lisa Marie Presley, and several clips of Elvis speaking. In 2008, Graceland opened two new exhibits: "Private Presley" focuses on the King's service in the army, and "Elvis '68" is about the year 1968 in Presley's life and musical career.

The exhibits gloss over some of the challenges Elvis faced in his life—his addiction to prescription drugs, his womanizing and failed marriage, and his unsettling affinity for firearms among them. But they showcase Elvis's generosity, his dedication to family, and his fun-loving character. The portrait

© ANDREA ZUCKER/MEMPHIS VISITORS BUREAU

It's a jungle in there: Graceland's Jungle Room.

that emerges is sympathetic and remarkably human for a man who is so often portrayed as larger than life.

The automobile museum features 33 vehicles, including his pink Cadillac, motorcycles, and a red MG from *Blue Hawaii,* as well as some of his favorite motorized toys, including a go-kart and dune buggy. His private planes include the *Lisa Marie,* which Elvis customized with gold-plated seat belts, suede chairs, and gold-flecked sinks. Other special Graceland exhibits include "Sincerely Elvis," which chronicles Elvis's life in 1956, and "Elvis After Dark," which describes some of Elvis's late-night passions, like roller skating.

The Graceland mansion was declared a National Historic Site in 2006. It attracts more than 650,000 visitors annually.

◀ Elmwood Cemetery

Elmwood Cemetery (824 S. Dudley St., 901/774-3212, www.elmwoodcemetery.org, daily 8 A.M.–4:30 P.M.), an 88-acre cemetery southwest of the city center, is the resting place of 70,000 Memphians—ordinary citizens and some of the city's most prominent leaders. It was founded in 1852 by 50 gentlemen who wanted the cemetery to be a park for the living as well as a resting place for the dead. They invested in tree planting and winding carriage paths so that the cemetery today is a pleasant, peaceful place to spend a few hours.

The cemetery is the resting place of Memphians like Annie Cook, a well-known madame who died during the yellow fever epidemic of 1878; Marion Scudder Griffen, a pioneering female lawyer and suffragette; and musician Sister Thea Bowman. Thousands of anonymous victims of the yellow fever epidemic were buried here, as were both Confederate and Union casualties of the Civil War. Prominent citizens including Robert Church Sr., Edward Hull Crump, and Shelby Foote are also buried at Elmwood.

Visitors to the cemetery may simply drive or walk through on their own. But it is best to rent the one-hour audio guide ($10) of the cemetery, which takes you on a driving tour and highlights 50 people buried in the cemetery. Thanks to a well-written and well-presented narration, the cemetery tour comes closer than any other single Memphis attraction to bringing Memphis's diverse history and people to life.

The cemetery offers occasional lectures and docent-guided tours for $15. Call ahead or check the website to find out if any are scheduled during your visit. To find Elmwood, drive east along E. H. Crump Boulevard, turning south (right) onto Dudley, which dead-ends at the single-lane bridge that marks the entrance to the cemetery.

Church of the Full Gospel Tabernacle

A native of Arkansas and longtime resident of Michigan, Al Green first made his name as one of history's greatest soul singers with hits like "Let's Stay Together," "Take Me to the River," and "Love and Happiness." Following a religious conversion in 1979, he dedicated his considerable talents to God and founded the Church of the Full Gospel Tabernacle (787 Hale Rd., 901/396-9192, www.algreenmusic.com) in Memphis, where his Sunday sermons dripped with soulful gospel.

For almost 11 years, the Reverend Al Green left secular music, dedicating himself to God's music. He began his return to secular music in 1988 and in 1995 Green released the first of three new secular albums on Blue Note Records.

According to his official biography, Rev. Green faced some criticism when he returned to the secular scene. "I've got people in the church saying, 'That's a secular song,' and I'm saying, 'Yeah, but you've got Monday, Tuesday, Wednesday, Thursday, Friday, and Saturday to be anything other than spiritual. You've got to live those days, too!'" Rev. Green says he has not neglected his duty to God. "The music is the message, the message is the music. So that's my

An angel watches over 70,000 Memphians in Elmwood Cemetery.

little ministry that the Big Man upstairs gave to me—a little ministry called love and happiness."

Despite his rebirth as a secular soul performer, Al Green, now a bishop, still makes time for his church. He preaches regularly, but not every Sunday, and continues to sing the praises of God. The Sunday service at his Memphis church begins at 11:30 A.M. Visitors are welcome, and you can come—within reason—as you are. Please show respect, though, by being quiet when that's called for and throwing a few bucks in the offering plate when it comes around. And don't forget that the church is a place of worship and not a tourist attraction. If you're not in town on Sunday, you can catch the weekly choir rehearsal on Thursday at 7 P.M.

National Ornamental Metal Museum

An unusual delight, the National Ornamental Metal Museum (374 Metal Museum Dr., 901/774-6380, www.metalmuseum.org, Tues.–Sat. 10 A.M.–5 P.M., Sun. noon–5 P.M., adults $6, seniors $5, students and children $4) is dedicated to preserving and displaying fine metalwork. Its permanent collection numbers more than 3,000 objects and ranges from contemporary American sculpture to works up to 500 years old. The museum hosts special exhibits several times a year, showcasing various aspects of metalwork. There is also a working metalwork studio, and the museum grounds on the bluff overlooking the Mississippi are an attraction in themselves. This is reputed to be the site where Hernando de Soto and his men camped when they passed through the area in 1542.

C. H. Nash Museum Chucalissa

A group of platform and ridge mounds along the Mississippi River are the main attraction at **Chucalissa Archaeological Site** (T. O. Fuller State Park, 901/678-2000, Tues.–Sat. 9 A.M.–5 P.M., adults $5, seniors and children $3). The mounds were once part of a Choctaw Indian community that existed A.D. 1000–1550. The village was empty when Europeans arrived, and the name Chucalissa means abandoned house.

The largest mound would have been where the chief and his family lived. The present-day museum, operated by the University of Memphis, consists of an exhibit about the Native Americans of the area and self-guided tour around the mounds and courtyard area, where games and meetings would have been held. There is also a half-mile nature trail along the bluff overlooking the river.

EAST MEMPHIS

East Memphis is home to old suburbs, gracious homes, and some excellent parks and other attractions.

The Dixon Gallery and Gardens

The Dixon Gallery and Gardens (4339 Park

Ave., 901/761-5250, www.dixon.org, Tues.–Fri. 10 A.M.–4 P.M., Sat. 10 A.M.–5 P.M., Sun. 1–5 P.M., adults $7, seniors $5, children $3), an art museum housed inside a stately Georgian-style home, has an impressive permanent collection of more than 2,000 paintings, many of them French impressionist and postimpressionist style, including works by Monet, Renoir, Degas, and Cézanne. It also mounts a half dozen special exhibits each year; previous ones have showcased the art of George Rodrigue and David Macaulay.

The Dixon is an easy place to spend several hours, immersed first in art and then in walking the paths that explore the house's 17 acres of beautifully tended gardens. There is a cutting garden, woodland garden, and formal gardens, among others.

Admission to the Dixon is free on Saturday 10 A.M.–noon and pay what you wish on Tuesday.

Memphis Botanic Garden

The 100-acre Memphis Botanic Garden (750 Cherry Rd., 901/636-4100, www.memphisbotanicgarden.com, summer daily 9 A.M.–6 P.M., winter daily 9 A.M.–4:30 P.M., adults $8, seniors $6.50, children $5) is home to more than 140 different species of trees and more than two dozen specialty gardens, including a Sculpture Garden, Azalea Trail, and Iris Garden. Trails meander through the gardens, but for the greatest fun buy a handful of fish food and feed the fish and ducks that inhabit the pond at the Japanese Garden. The garden puts on a number of events, including blockbuster concerts, workshops, plant sales, and programs for children.

The Pink Palace

A good destination for families, the Pink Palace (3050 Central Ave., 901/636-2362, www.memphismuseums.org, Mon.–Sat. 9 A.M.–5 P.M., Sun. noon–5 P.M.) is a group of attractions rolled into one. The **Pink Palace Museum** (adults $9.75, seniors $9.25, children $6.25) is a museum about Memphis, with exhibits about the natural history of the Mid-South

region and the city's development. There is a full-scale replica of the first Piggly Wiggly grocery market, plus an exhibit about how health care became such a large part of the Memphis economy. The museum is housed within the Pink Palace Mansion, the Memphis home of Piggly Wiggly founder Clarence Saunders.

The Pink Palace is also home to the **Sharpe Planetarium** (Tues.–Sat., adults $4.50, seniors and children $4) and an IMAX movie theater (adults $8.25, seniors $7.50, children $6.50), which shows movies daily. Special package tickets are available for all the Pink Palace attractions.

Art Museum of the University of Memphis

The Art Museum of the University of Memphis (142 CFA Building, 901/678-2224, www.memphis.edu/amum, Mon.–Sat. 9 A.M.–5 P.M., free) houses excellent but small exhibits of ancient Egyptian and African art and artifacts, and a noteworthy print gallery. There are frequent special exhibitions. The museum is closed during university holidays and in between temporary exhibits.

Children's Museum of Memphis

You will know the Children's Museum of Memphis (2525 Central Ave., 901/458-2678, www.cmom.com, daily 9 A.M.–5 P.M., $12) by the large alphabet blocks outside spelling its acronym, CMOM. Bring children here for constructive and educational play: They can sit in a flight simulator and real airplane cockpit, climb through the arteries of a model heart, climb a skyscraper, and more. The museum has 26 permanent exhibits and several traveling exhibits.

Lichterman Nature Center

Lichterman Nature Center (5992 Quince Rd., 901/767-7322, Tues.–Thurs. 10 A.M.–3 P.M., Fri.–Sat. 10 A.M.–4 P.M., adults $6, children $4.50) is dedicated to generating interest and enthusiasm for the Mid-South's nature. The park encompasses some 65 acres, and visitors will enjoy seeing native trees and flowers, including dogwood, lotus, and pine. There is a museum about the local environment, picnic facilities, and pleasant trails. Environmental education is the center's mission, and this certified arboretum is a popular destination for families and school groups.

TOURS
History Tours
Heritage Tours Memphis (901/527-3427, adults $33, youth 12–17 $25, children under 11 $23) is the city's only tour company dedicated to presenting Memphis's African American history. Operated by Memphians Elaine Turner and Joan Nelson, Heritage Tours offers black heritage, musical heritage, civil rights, and Beale Street walking tours. They can also arrange out-of-town tours to area attractions, such as the Alex Haley home in Henning, Tennessee. Most local tours cost $25 and last about three hours.

The black heritage tour starts at the W. C. Handy Home and Museum and includes a stop at the Slavehaven Underground Railroad Museum, plus narration that tells the story of black Memphians such as Ida B. Wells, Robert Church, and Tom Lee, and the events leading up to the assassination of Dr. Martin Luther King Jr. You will drive past the Mason Temple Church of God in Christ at 930 Mason Street, where Dr. King gave his famous "mountaintop" speech the night before his death.

River Tours
The **Memphis Queen Riverboat Tours** (901/527-2628, www.memphisriverboats.net, adults $20, seniors, college students, military children 13–17 $17, children 4–12 $10, toddlers $5) leave daily at 2:30 P.M. from the Port of Memphis, located at the foot of Monroe Avenue on the riverfront. The afternoon tour lasts 90 minutes and takes you a few miles south of the city before turning around. Commentary tells some of the most famous tales of the river, but the biggest attraction of the tour is simply being on Old Man River. The views of the Memphis skyline from the water are impressive. Concessions are available onboard. The riverboats also offer dinner cruises at 7:30 P.M. with live music for about $45 per person. See website to check dates and times.

Music Tours
Memphis just looks better from the passenger window of a 1955 Cadillac. That's as good a reason as any to call Tad Pierson for one of his **American Dream Safari** (901/527-8870, www.americandreamsafari.com, $40 with five passengers) tours of Memphis. Pierson offers tours with a difference—he does not just do sightseeing; he promises experiences and memories for his guests. His tours include juke joints of Memphis, gospel churches, a Mississippi Delta day trip, a special tour for photographers, plus much more. Pierson really gets the unique appeal of Memphis, and he wants to share it with his guests.

Music-themed tours are the specialty at **Backbeat Tours** (800/979-3370, www.backbeattours.com, $13–45, tickets must be reserved in advance). You will travel on a reconditioned 1959 transit bus and be serenaded by live musicians. Tours include the Memphis Mojo Tour (adults $33, students $31, children 12–17 $19), which takes you to Memphis music landmarks like Sun Studio and the Stax Museum, and the Hound Dog tour, which follows in Elvis Presley's Memphis footsteps. Backbeat can also take you to Graceland and offers two walking tours of Memphis—a Memphis Ghost Tour ($20) and "The Dark Side of Memphis" ($13) which explores the bloody and creepy side of history—on Wednesday through Sunday evenings.

MEMPHIS

Entertainment and Events

Memphis's vibrant, diverse personality is reflected in its entertainment scene. Blues, rap, R&B, and gospel are just some of the types of music you can hear on any given weekend. Alternative and indie rock finds a receptive audience in Memphis, as does opera, Broadway productions, and the symphony. There's always a good excuse to go out.

LIVE MUSIC AND CLUBS

Memphis may be the birthplace of the blues, but there's a lot more to the music scene than that. It's true that you can catch live blues at a Beale Street nightclub or in a city juke joint. But you can also find hard-edge rock, jazz, and acoustic music most nights of the week. The best resource for up-to-date entertainment listings is the free weekly *Memphis Flyer* (www.memphisflyer.com), which comes out on Wednesday morning and includes a detailed listing of club dates and concerts.

Keep in mind that big-name artists often perform at casinos in Tunica, just over the state line in Mississippi. Many of these shows are advertised in Memphis media outlets, or check out the upcoming events on the Tunica Convention and Visitors Bureau website, www.tunicamiss.com.

Blues

One of the first things you should do when you get to Memphis is to find out if the **Center for Southern Folklore** (119 S. Main St., 901/525-3655, www.southernfolklore.com, Mon.–Fri. 11 A.M.–5 P.M., Sat. 11 A.M.–6 P.M.) has any concerts or activities planned during your visit. The center has been documenting and preserving traditional Memphis and Delta blues music since the 1970s. They put on concerts and lectures, produce documentaries, offer group tours and educational programs, and organize the annual Memphis Music and Heritage Festival over Labor Day weekend. They often have live blues on Friday afternoon and offer a variety of special shows. This is one of the best places to hear authentic blues. The center has a 250-seat dining room and performance space in Peabody Place, as well as a folklore store that sells folk art, books, CDs, and hot peach cobbler, among other things. A sign stating "Be Nice or Leave" sets the tone as soon as you step into this colorful and eclectic shop, one of the best gift shops in the city. The center is a nonprofit organization and well worth supporting.

Beale Street is ground zero for Memphis's blues music scene. While some people lament that Beale has become a sad tourist trap, it can still be a worthwhile place to spend your evening. Indeed, no other part of Memphis has as much music and entertainment packed into such a small area. On a typical night, Beale Street is packed with a diverse crowd strolling from one bar to the next. Beer seems to run a close second to music as the street's prime attraction, with many bars selling directly onto the street through concession windows. The "Big Ass Beer" cups used by many establishments say it all.

Nearly all Beale Street bars have live music, but one of the most popular is **B. B. King's Blues Club** (143 Beale St., 901/524-5464, cover $5–7), owned by the legend himself. B. B. King performs here two or three times a year—keep your ear to the ground since the shows are not usually advertised. On other evenings, local acts and some nationally known performers take the stage. B. B. King's draws a mostly tourist crowd, and it is a chain, but with the blues on full throttle, you probably won't care too much.

Also on Beale Street, **Blues City Cafe** (138 Beale St., 901/526-3637, cover $3–5) books blues, plus a variety of other acts including

MEMPHIS JUKE JOINTS

In Memphis, there are only two reasons to go to a juke joint full of blues: because you feel good or because you feel bad. Beale Street is a reliable source seven nights a week, and your visit to Memphis wouldn't be complete without checking out its scene. But if you want to sneak away from the tourist crowd and catch some homegrown talent, check out a real Memphis juke joint. Live music is typical on Friday and Saturday nights and sometimes Sunday, but it gets scarce during the week. Generally music starts late (11 P.M.) and finishes early (3 A.M.). Don't be surprised if the person you've engaged in conversation sitting next to you gets called to the stage sometime during the evening and delivers a beautiful song.

Remember that it's in the nature of things for these clubs to come and go. The following listings were current as of this writing, but they are always subject to change.

- **Wild Bill's** (1580 Vollentine St., 901/726-5473): A legendary club in Memphis. The Patriarch himself passed away in the summer of 2007, but what he established will still carry on. The quintessential juke joint. Small, intimate, an open kitchen serving chicken wings, and ice-cold beer served in 40-ounce bottles. Home to Ms. Nikki and the Memphis Soul Survivors.

- **CC's Blues Club** (1427 Thomas St., 901/526-5566): More upscale. More mirrors. But a great dance floor, and don't you dare come underdressed. Security guards patrol the parking lot.

- **Mr. Handy's Blues Hall** (182 Beale St., 901/528-0150): New Orleans has Preservation Hall. Memphis has Handy's Blues Hall. Everyone bad-raps Beale Street and its jangly tourism scene, but if you catch it on a good night when Dr. Feelgood warms up his harmonica and you look around the room at the memorabilia on the walls, you could be in a joint at the end of a country road in Mississippi.

- **The Blue Worm** (1405 Airways Dr., 901/327-7947): When a legendary juke joint band gets old and disintegrates, this is where it ends up. The Fieldstones have been *the* band in Memphis since the early '60s. Now it's down to Wilroy Sanders, the Last Living Bluesman. The house band can get behind anybody and make them a superstar, for one glorious song.

- **Big S Bar and Grill** (1179 Dunnavant Ave., 901/775-9127): They say blues is a feeling. The Big S doesn't have live music, but if you want to sink into the atmosphere of a bar that's dark with mystery and history plus the warmest vibe in town, come on home. Blues DJ on Sunday nights, and the jukebox is a veritable encyclopedia of blues.

- **The Boss** (912 Jackson Ave., 901/522-8883): Thursday nights only. Ever heard the overused phrase "best-kept secret in town"? Jesse Dotson on piano. Leroy Hodges on bass. Roy Cunningham on drums. An array of singers like Preacher Man, Bill Coday, O. T. Sykes. Now you don't have to wait for the weekend.

---

doo-wop, zydeco, R&B, funk, and "high-impact rockabilly." The café-restaurant is one of the most popular on Beale Street, and its nightclub, **Rum Boogie Cafe** (rumboogie.com, cover $3–5), has an award-winning house band, James Covan and the Boogie Blues Band, that performs most evenings.

Jazz

If you want a break from the blues, **King's Palace Cafe** (162 Beale St., 901/521-1851, www.kingspalacecafe.com) specializes in jazz. Lots of wood paneling and red paint make the bar and Cajun restaurant warm and welcoming. This is an unpretentious place to have a meal or listen to live music. There is a $1 per person entertainment charge when you sit at a table.

On South Main, **Café Soul** (492 S. Main St., 901/859-0557, cover varies) has live jazz, gospel, or soul most nights of the week, good for a relaxing evening after browsing the galleries.

MEMPHIS

Rock

Still on Beale Street, **Alfred's** (197 Beale St., 901/525-3711, www.alfredsonbeale.com, cover $5 Fri. and Sat.) has rock acts five nights a week. On Sunday evening, the 17-piece Memphis Jazz Orchestra takes the stage. The dance floor at Alfred's is one of the best on Beale Street.

One of Beale Street's most historic nightclubs, **The New Daisy** (330 Beale St., 901/525-8979, cover $5 and up) books rock 'n' roll, independent, and a few R&B acts. There are shows most nights of the week; call ahead or check the entertainment listings for a schedule. The Daisy is an all-ages club, and many shows attract a young audience.

Off Beale Street, the **Hi-Tone Cafe** (1913 Poplar Ave., 901/278-8663, www.hitone-memphis.com, cover varies) is probably the best place to see live music in town. The Hi-Tone books all kinds of acts, from high-energy rockers to soulful acoustic acts. They are really committed to bringing good live music to Memphis. The cover charge for local shows is a few bucks, but tickets for bigger-name acts can run $20 and more. The bar serves respectable burgers and finger foods, excellent martinis, and lots of beer.

Also in midtown, **The Buccaneer** (1368 Monroe, 901/278-0909, cover varies) books rock acts most days a week. Cover charge rarely tops $5.

BARS
Downtown

You can head to Beale Street for a night out, regardless of whether or not you sing the blues.

The best place to grab a beer downtown is the **Beale Street Tap Room** (168 Beale St., 901/527-4392). With more than 30 beers on tap, this is a great choice for beer lovers. The service is friendly and low-key, and regulars have their own mug.

Off Beale Street, **The Peabody Hotel Memphis** (149 Union Ave., 901/529-4000, www.peabodymemphis.com) may be the best place to enjoy a relaxing drink. The lobby bar offers good service, comfortable seats, and an unrivaled atmosphere.

In Peabody Place about a block from Beale Street, **The Flying Saucer Draught Emporium** (130 Peabody Pl., 901/523-8536, www.beerknurd.com) draws a lively happy-hour crowd. The bar offers more than 75 draft beers, plus cocktails and wine. Grab a seat along the windows and watch downtown Memphis come alive as the sun sets.

In the South Main district, **Ernestine and Hazel's** (531 S. Main St., 901/523-9754) is one of Memphis's most celebrated pit stops for cold drinks and a night out. Once a brothel, Ernestine and Hazel's now has one of the best jukeboxes in town. Take a seat upstairs in one of the old brothel rooms and watch South Main Street below. Rumor is the joint is haunted, but folks come here for the jukebox, not the spirits.

Midtown

The **Young Avenue Deli** (2119 Young Ave., 901/278-3123, www.youngavenuedeli.com) is a friendly neighborhood bar that books occasional live acts. Located in the hip Cooper-Young neighborhood, Young Avenue Deli has hundreds of different beers on tap or in bottles. The bar attracts a diverse crowd, from young hipsters to older neighborhood denizens.

A favorite place for music, pool, and a night out in midtown is the **Blue Monkey** (2012 Madison Ave., 901/272-2583, www.bluemonkeymemphis.com). Grab a pizza and a beer, shoot some pool, and then rock out to the live band.

Murphy's (1589 Madison Ave., 901/726-4193) is a neighborhood bar with a nice patio.

Perfect for a business date or after-work pit stop, **The Grove Grill** (4550 Poplar Ave., 901/818-9951, www.thegrovegrill.com) is popular with businesspeople and office workers.

Two of Memphis's best sports bars are found in the eastern reaches of the city. **Brookhaven Pub & Grill** (695 W. Brookhaven

© HENRYK SADURA/123RF.COM

The Orpheum Theatre at Main and Beale is one of the city's major arts venues.

Cir., 901/680-8118, www.brookhavenpuband-grill.com) has big-screen plasma televisions, great beer on tap, and lots of fans. Tuesday night is quiz night. **Gill's Bar & Grill** (551 S. Highland, 901/458-2787), near the University of Memphis, specializes in cold beers and sports, and has a great happy hour.

GAY AND LESBIAN NIGHTLIFE

Many Memphis gay and lesbian clubs don't get going until late night, after other clubs have closed.

Metro Memphis (1349 Autumn Ave., 901/274-8010, cover varies) is a gay bar and dance club that attracts both gay and straight patrons.

The city's largest dance floor may be found at **Backstreet Memphis** (2018 Court Ave., 901/276-5522, cover varies), a midtown club that has light shows, drag shows, karaoke, and other high-energy entertainment.

A nightclub institution in midtown, **J Wags Bar** (1268 Madison Ave., 901/278-4313, cover varies) doesn't usually get going until the wee

hours, after other mainstream clubs have closed. It claims to be Memphis's oldest gay and lesbian bar.

THE ARTS

Memphis has a growing arts scene. The **Greater Memphis Arts Council** (901/578-2787, www.artsmemphis.org) provides funding for more than 20 local arts groups and is a good source of information about upcoming events.

Major arts venues include the **Cannon Center for the Performing Arts** (255 N. Main St., 901/576-1200, www.thecannoncenter.com) and the **Orpheum Theatre** (Main and Beale Sts., 901/525-3000, www.orpheum-memphis. com). They regularly book major artists and Broadway performances.

Theater

For theater, check out **Playhouse on the Square** (66 S. Cooper St., 901/726-4656, www.play-houseonthesquare.org). This dynamic Memphis institution serves as home to several of the city's acting companies and puts on 15–20 different performances every year. It also offers theater classes, school performances, and pay-what-you-can shows. The playhouse also screens classic movies on the first Sunday of each month.

Theatre Memphis (630 Perkins Ext., 901/682-8323, www.theatrememphis.org) is a community theater company that has been in existence since the 1920s. They stage about 12 shows annually at their theater in midtown.

TheatreWorks (2085 Monroe Ave., 901/274-7139, www.theatreworksmemphis.org) encourages nontraditional and new theater with organizations including Our Own Voice Theatre Troupe, the Memphis Black Repertory Theatre, and the Playwright's Forum.

Music

The **Memphis Symphony Orchestra** (585 S. Mendenhall Rd., 901/537-2525, www.memphis-symphony.org) performs on a varied calendar of works year-round in its home at the Cannon Center for the Performing Arts at 2155 North Main Street. The symphony was founded in 1952 and today has more than 850 musicians, staff, and volunteers.

Opera

Opera Memphis (6745 Wolf River Blvd., 901/257-3100, www.operamemphis.org) performs traditional opera at a variety of venues around town, including the historic Orpheum Theatre on Beale Street and the Germantown Performing Arts Centre.

Dance

Ballet Memphis (901/737-7322, www.balletmemphis.org) performs classical dance at the Playhouse on the Square and other venues throughout the city. The **New Ballet Ensemble** (901/726-9225, www.newballet.org) puts on performances around the city with "dancers in do-rags as well as tights," in the words of the *Commercial Appeal.*

Project Motion (TheatreWorks, 2085 Monroe Ave., 901/274-7139, www.projectmotiondance.org) is a contemporary dance collective that performs innovative works.

Cinemas

There are a half dozen multiscreen movie theaters in and around Memphis. For independent movies, try **Malco's Paradiso** (584 S. Mendenhall Rd., 901/682-1754, www.malco.com) or **Studio on the Square** (2105 Court St., 901/725-7151, www.malco.com). In the summer, check out the **Orpheum** (203 S. Main St., 901/525-3000) for classic movies, and the **Malco Summer 4 Drive-In** (5310 Summer Ave., 901/681-2020) for a drive-in experience.

FESTIVALS AND EVENTS
Spring

Memphians celebrate their African heritage over a long weekend in mid-April. **Africa in April** (901/947-2133, www.africainapril.org) honors a specific country in Africa each year; activities include cooking, storytelling, music, and a parade. The festival takes place at Church Park on the east end of Beale Street.

In early May, the Memphis-based Blues Foundation hosts the annual **Handy Awards** (www.blues.org), the Grammys of the blues world.

Memphis in May (www.memphisinmay.org), the city's largest annual event, is really three major festivals rolled into one. The **Beale Street Music Festival,** which takes place at Tom Lee Park on the river during the first weekend of May, kicks things off with a celebration of Memphis music. Expect a lot of wow performers, plus many more up-and-coming talents. The festival has grown over the years, and it is now a three-day event with four stages of music going simultaneously. In addition to music, the festival offers excellent people-watching, lots of barbecue, cold beer, and festivity. You can buy daily tickets or a three-day pass for the whole weekend.

In mid-May, attention turns to the **World Championship Barbeque Cooking Contest,** a celebration of pork, pigs, and barbecue that takes place in Tom Lee Park. In addition to the barbecue judging, there is entertainment, hog-calling contests, and other piggy antics. If you're not part of a competing team (or friends with one), you can buy barbecue from vendors who set up in the park.

Finally, at the end of the month, there is the **Memphis International Festival,** which pays tribute to a different country each year with presentations about its music, food, culture, and history.

Book your hotel rooms early for Memphis in May, since many hotels, particularly those downtown, sell out.

Summer

Carnival Memphis (901/458-2500, www.carnivalmemphis.org) takes place in June. The Carnival features a parade and fireworks. This festival, once called Cotton Carnival, was segregated for decades, but since the mid-1980s has been racially integrated.

The annual candlelight vigil at Graceland on August 15, the anniversary of Elvis's death, has grown into a whole week of Elvis-centric activities throughout Memphis. More than 30,000 people visit Graceland during **Elvis Week** (www.elvisweek.com), and during the vigil his most adoring fans walk solemnly up the Graceland drive to pay their respects at his grave. Special concerts, tribute shows, and movies are shown during the week as the city celebrates its most famous export even more than usual.

Fall

Organized by the Center for Southern Folklore, the **Memphis Music and Heritage Festival** (901/525-3655, www.southernfolklore.com), held over Labor Day weekend, sticks close to the roots of Memphis music. Performers include gospel singers, bona fide bluesmen and women, rockabilly superstars, and much more.

Performances take place in the center's shop and concert hall on Main Street, making them more intimate than other blockbuster music festivals.

End-of-summer fairs are a tradition for Southern and rural communities all over the United States. The 10-day **Mid-South Fair** (www.midsouthfair.org) in September is a bonanza of attractions: livestock shows, rodeos, agricultural judging, concerts, beauty pageants, exhibitions, carnival rides, funnel cakes, and cotton candy. In 2008 it moved from the Mid-South Fairgrounds in southeast Memphis to a 150-acre site across the road from the Tunica, Mississippi, Welcome Center, about 30 miles from Memphis.

In mid-September, the Cooper-Young neighborhood throws its annual jamboree at the **Cooper-Young Festival** (www.cooperyoungfestival.com). There is an arts and crafts fair, live music, and food vendors at this street carnival.

The annual **Southern Heritage Classic** (www.southernheritageclassic.com) is one of the South's big football games. But the match of two historically black college rivals, Jackson State University and Tennessee State University, is more than just a game; it is a serious city-wide festival.

Forty-six-foot long boats with dragon heads and tails race at Mud Island River Park each September during the **Duncan-Williams Dragon Boat Races** (www.memphis.racedragonboats.com).

Winter

The colder weather welcomes a number of sporting events, including the **St. Jude Marathon and Half Marathon** (www.stjudemarathon.org, 800/565-5112) in December, which is a qualifying race for the Boston Marathon. The **AutoZone Liberty Bowl** (www.libertybowl.org, 901/795-7700) typically welcomes two of the NCAA's best football teams to town on New Year's Eve.

Taking place over the weekend closest to Elvis Presley's January 8 birthday, the **Elvis**

Birthday Celebration (www.elvis.com) draws Elvis fans with special performances, dance parties, and a ceremony at Graceland proclaiming Elvis Presley Day.

The two-day **Beale Street Zydeco Music Festival** (901/619-5865) takes place over the last weekend in February and features more than 20 bands paying tribute to Cajun music.

Shopping

GIFTS AND SOUVENIRS

Any of the half dozen gift shops along Beale Street sell gifts and souvenirs of the city. **Memphis Music** (149 Beale St., 901/526-5047) has a good selection of CDs and DVDs for music fans. For a unique gift or something practical for yourself, **A. Schwab** (163 Beale St., 901/523-9782) is your best choice, and lots of fun to boot.

Another good place for gift shopping is the **Center for Southern Folklore** (123 S. Main St., 901/525-3655), which has books, art, and music focusing on the region. All of the city's museums have good gift shops, including the National Civil Rights Museum, **Stax Museum of American Soul Music,** and **Sun Studio,** where everything is emblazoned with the distinctive yellow Sun label.

If you have a car, head out to **Shangri-La Records** (1916 Madison Ave., 901/274-1916, www.shangri.com), one of the city's best record stores, which specializes in Memphis music. **Goner Records** (2152 Young Ave., 901/722-0095, www.goner-records.com) is both a record store and a record label.

If the gift recipient in your life is a fashion maven, head to **Thigh High Jeans** (525 N.

Nab a soul souvenir at the Stax Museum of American Soul Music.

© DAN BALL/MEMPHIS VISITORS BUREAU

Main, www.thighhighjeans.com) where you can buy embroidered skirts and newly remade jeans created from recycled denim. A percentage of each purchase is donated to the charity of the shopper's choice.

ART

For art boutiques and galleries, head south to the South Main arts district, where you will find galleries including **D'Edge Art and Unique Treasures** (550 S. Main St., 901/521-0054), which has contemporary folk art, and **Robinson Gallery/Archives** (44 Huling Ave., 901/619-4478, www.robinsongallery.com), a photography gallery that houses the work of *Vogue* photographer Jack Robinson Jr.

On the last Friday of each month the trolleys are free, the galleries stay open, and hundreds of arts-minded Memphians head to South Main to mingle into the night. For a directory of all South Main galleries, contact the **South Main Association** (901/578-7262, www.south-mainmemphis.net).

Since 2003 the **Wings Gallery** (100 N. Humphreys Blvd., 901/322-2984) has shown the work of artists whose lives have been impacted by cancer. Exhibitions change every six weeks.

ANTIQUES

Head out Central Avenue, to the area between Cooper and East Parkway, for the greatest concentration of antiques stores. **Flashback** (2304 Central Ave., 901/272-2304, www.flashback-memphis.com) sells both vintage furniture and clothes, including a whole lot of Levi's jeans. Another good choice is **Toad Hall Antiques** (2129 Central Ave., 901/726-0755, www.toadhallmemphis.com), easy to find because of a brightly painted mural on the outside of the building.

THRIFT STORES

In a city where vintage never went out of style, you can expect excellent thrift stores. The biggest and best is **AmVets** (2526 Elvis Presley Blvd., 901/775-5018). You can also try the Junior League of Memphis's **Repeat Boutique Thrift Store** (3586 Summer Ave., 901/327-4777).

In a city of characters, the most colorful shopping experience in Memphis is found at **The Memphis Flea Market–The Big One** (in the AgriCenter, 7777 Walnut Grove Rd., 901/752-8441, www.memphisfleamarket.com), which takes place the third weekend of each month at the Mid-South Fairgrounds. Between 800 and 1,000 vendors turn up each month with housewares, clothing, computers, jewelry, antiques, yard art, and so much more. Between 20,000 and 25,000 people come to shop. Admission is $3 for adults, free for kids. Parking is free.

SHOPPING MALLS

The most upscale shopping mall in the Memphis area is **Wolfchase Galleria** (2760 N. Germantown Pkwy., 901/372-9409). Located in Cordova, an east-lying suburb now consumed by Memphis sprawl, the galleria celebrated its 10th anniversary in 2007. It is aging gracefully, with national retailers including Brooks Brothers, Abercrombie & Fitch, and Sephora. Department stores at the mall include Macy's, Dillard's, Sears, and JCPenney. You can take either exit 16 or 18 off I-40 to get to Wolfchase Galleria.

Also in Germantown, the swanky **Shops of Saddle Creek** (7509 Poplar Ave., 901/753-4264) has Williams-Sonoma, Banana Republic, and an Apple computer store, among others.

Closer to the city center, **Oak Court Mall** (4465 Poplar Ave., 901/682-8928) was the location of the very first Starbucks in Tennessee. It is also consistently voted Memphians' favorite mall, no doubt because it offers a good selection of stores in a pleasant atmosphere, and it's relatively close to town. Department stores at Oak Court include Macy's and Dillard's; the mall also has Aveda, Jos A. Bank, Banana Republic, and dozens more stores.

And if that's not enough for you, head across the road to **Laurelwood Shopping Center** (Poplar Ave. at Perkins Ext., 901/794-6022), where you'll find specialty clothing and shoe boutiques, as well special events like free yoga classes.

In South Memphis, **Southland Mall** (1215 Southland Mall, 901/346-7664) is Memphis's oldest mall. Built in 1966, Southland soldiers on. There is a Sears, as well as specialty shops including Radio Shack and Bath & Body Works.

OUTLET SHOPPING

You can buy directly from name-brand retailers at rock-bottom prices at the **Lakeland Factory Outlet Mall** (3536 Canada Rd., 901/388-5707). Located at the Canada Road exit off I-40, the mall boasts a number of national retailers, including Bass, Van Heusen, Dress Barn, Toy Liquidators, and Old Time Pottery, which sells discounted dinnerware, garden goods, and other housewares.

Sports and Recreation

With a professional basketball team, excellent downtown baseball club, and lots of city parks, Memphis is a great city in which to both watch sports and get active yourself.

PARKS
Downtown

Named for the legendary blues composer, **Handy Park,** on Beale Street, between 3rd Street and Rufus Thomas Boulevard, seems a tad out of place among Beale's nightclubs and restaurants. But the park is a site of historical importance, if only because of the statue of its namesake that guards its gates. The park hosts occasional outdoor concerts and festivals, and at other times you will find places to sit and a handful of vendors.

Uptown

Tom Lee Park, a long, narrow grassy park that overlooks the Mississippi, is a popular venue for summertime festivals and events. It is also used year-round for walking and jogging, and by people who simply want to look out at the giant river. The park is named for Tom Lee, an African American man who saved the lives of 32 people when the steamboat they were on sank in the river in 1925. Lee, who pulled people out of the river and into his boat, "Zev," could not even swim. An outmoded monument erected at the park in 1954 calls Lee "a very worthy negro."

Located on the northern side of downtown Memphis, **Court Square,** three blocks from the waterfront along Court Avenue, is a pleasant city park surrounded by historic buildings. Court Square is one of four parks that was included when the city was first planned in 1819. There are benches and trees, and it is a wireless Internet hot spot.

Confederate Park, located on Front Street between Court and Jefferson Streets, commemorates Confederate soldiers who died in the Battle of Memphis, as well as other war dead. There is a statue of Jefferson Davis in the center of the park. This is where many Memphians gathered to watch the Battle of Memphis in 1862, and it remains a good place to view the river below.

Midtown

Located in midtown Memphis, **Overton Park** (1928 Poplar Ave.) is one of the best all-around parks the city has to offer. This 342-acre park has a nine-hole golf course, nature trails through the woods, bike trails, an outdoor amphitheater now called the Levitt Shell, and lots of green, open spaces. The park shares space with the Memphis Zoo and the Memphis Brooks Museum of Art, making the area a popular destination for city residents and visitors.

The Madison Avenue trolley passes **Forrest Park,** along Madison Avenue, between North

Manassas and North Dunlap Streets, an ample city park dedicated to the memory of the controversial Nathan Bedford Forrest. Forrest, a slave trader, Confederate, and the first grand wizard of the Ku Klux Klan, has an uncomfortable position of prominence in Memphis and the whole of western Tennessee. Both he and his wife are buried in the park.

South Memphis

Southwest of the city center, about 15 minutes' drive from the airport, is **T. O. Fuller State Park** (1500 Mitchell Rd., 901/543-7581). The visitors center here is open weekdays 8 A.M.–sunset. Amenities at the 1,138-acre park include sheltered picnic areas, tennis courts, a golf course, swimming pool ($3), basketball courts, softball field, six miles of hiking trails, and camping facilities. T. O. Fuller State Park was the first state park east of the Mississippi River open to African Americans, and the second in the nation.

East Memphis

Located near the University of Memphis and Oak Court Mall, **Audubon Park** (4161 Park Ave.) has a golf course, tennis courts, walking trails, and other sports facilities. The Memphis Botanic Garden is located here.

Memphians celebrate the fact that their largest city park, **Shelby Farms** (www.shelbyfarmspark.org), is five times the size of New York's Central Park. But the fact is that Shelby Farms is underused, because most of its 4,500 acres are pleasantly undeveloped. There are plans to improve the park by adding more recreational facilities. However, more than 500,000 people come here annually to go mountain biking, horseback riding, inline skating, walking, or running along some of the many trails. You can also fish, raft, canoe, or sail on any of the park's six lakes. There is a wheelchair-accessible trail, areas for picnicking, and a shooting range. Shelby Farms was originally set aside to

be the county penal farm, and although it was not used in this way, the county jail is found on the western edge of the park. Shelby Farms is located on the eastern side of the city, just outside the I-40/I-240 loop that circles Memphis. It is easily accessible from exits 12 and 14 off I-40, and exit 13 off I-240. Or follow Walnut Grove Road from midtown.

BIKING

Most cyclists in the city bike as a form of recreation, rather than transportation. The City of Memphis has established five bike routes that circle the city and various neighborhoods. These routes are marked and have designated parking and restroom facilities at the start. They are not bike paths—you share the road with cars—and normal safety measures are necessary.

The **Memphis Hightailers Bicycle Club** (www.memphishightailers.com) organizes frequent rides for various levels, with distances ranging 20–100 miles. In addition, there are rides leaving every Saturday and Sunday at 8 A.M. from the Super-Lo parking lot at Southern Avenue and Colonial Street.

For bike rentals, gear, and advice about riding in and around the city, go to **Peddler Bike Shop** (575 S. Highland, 901/327-4833, www.peddlerbikeshop.com), where owner Hal Mabray will happily help you get geared up to ride. A used-bike rental will cost about $35 for a half day, $50 per day. Go for a long weekend for $100. There are also bikes for rent at Mud Island.

There are a number of parks near Memphis that are bike friendly. **Meeman-Shelby Forest State Park,** north of the city, has five miles of paved bike paths, and cyclists use the main park roads for more extensive riding. Bicyclists will also find trails at **Shelby Farms.**

It is also noteworthy that the **Mississippi River Trail,** a bicycle route that will eventually run from the headwaters of the Mississippi River in Minnesota to the Gulf of Mexico, runs from Reelfoot Lake in northeastern Tennessee, through

Memphis, and on to Mississippi. For maps and details, go to www.mississippirivertrail.org.

GOLF

The City of Memphis operates award-winning 18-hole golf courses at **Audubon Park** (4160 Park Ave., 901/683-6941), with gently rolling hills; **Fox Meadows** (3064 Clarke Rd., 901/362-0232), which is easy to walk but has several challenging holes; **Galloway Park** (3815 Walnut Grove, 901/685-7805); **Davy Crockett Golf Course** (4380 Rangeline Rd., 901/358-3375); and **Pine Hill Park** (1005 Alice Ave., 901/775-9434), a great course for walkers.

There are two public nine-hole courses: one at **Riverside Park** (465 S. Parkway W., 901/576-4296) and one at **Overton Park** (2080 Poplar Ave., 901/725-9905). Greens fees on the public courses are under $20.

One of the best-kept golf secrets in town is the 18-hole par 71 course at **T.O. Fuller State Park** (1500 W. Mitchell Rd., 901/543-7771), south of downtown. The semiprivate **Mirimichi** (6195 Woodstock Cuba Rd., 901/259-3800, www.mirimichi.com) in Millington is part-owned by heartthrob Justin Timberlake, a former Memphian. Millington is about a 30-minute drive from downtown.

TENNIS

The city operates public tennis courts at several parks, including **Bert Ferguson Park** (8505 Trinity), **Gaisman Park** (4223 Macon), **Glenview** (1141 Barksdale), **Martin Luther King Jr. Park** (South Pkwy. at Riverside Dr.), and **University Park** (University at Edward).

There are also four public indoor/outdoor tennis complexes: **Bellevue** (1239 Orgill Rd., 901/774-7199); **Leftwich** (4145 Southern, 901/685-7907); **Whitehaven,** also called Eldon Roark (1500 Finley Rd., 901/332-0546); and **Wolbrecht** (1645 Ridgeway, 901/767-2889). Fees vary per facility; call in advance for information and court reservations.

SWIMMING

The City of Memphis operates a dozen outdoor pools that are open June–August, and several indoor pools open year-round. Public outdoor pools are open Tuesday–Saturday 1–6 P.M., and admission is free. The outdoor pools include **L. E. Brown Pool** (617 S. Orleans, 901/527-3620), in southeastern Memphis; **Lester Pool** (317 Tillman Rd., 901/323-2261), in eastern Memphis; **Riverview Pool** (182 Joubert Rd., 901/948-7609), at Kansas Park in south Memphis; and **Willow Pool** (4777 Willow Rd., 901/763-2917). Expect crowds; Memphis gets hot in the summer.

Two indoor pools are open to the general public: the **Bickford Aquatic Center** (235 Henry Ave., 901/578-3732, Mon.–Fri. 10 A.M.–6 P.M.) and **Hickory Hill Aquatic Center** (3910 Ridgeway Rd., 901/566-9685, Mon., Wed., and Fri. 9 A.M.–8 P.M., Tues. and Thurs. 6–9 A.M. and noon–8 P.M., Sat. 9 A.M.–1 P.M.).

GYMS

Out-of-towners can get a day pass to the **Louis T. Fogelman Downtown YMCA** (245 Madison Ave., 901/527-9622, Mon.–Thurs. 5 A.M.–10 P.M., Fri. 5 A.M.–9 P.M., Sat. 8 A.M.–6 P.M., Sun. noon–6 P.M., day pass $10) and use the indoor pool and track, and extensive gym facilities. City residents can buy one of the membership packages.

SPECTATOR SPORTS
Basketball

In 2001, Memphis realized the dream of many in the Mid-South when the Vancouver Grizzlies announced they would be moving south. The NBA team played its first two seasons in Memphis at the Pyramid before the massive $250 million FedEx Forum opened for the 2004–2005 season. The arena is one of the largest in the NBA and hosts frequent concerts and performances by major artists.

The **Grizzlies** have yet to achieve any major

titles, but they went to the finals and play-offs in 2010–2011 and 2011–2012. Ticket prices range from under $20 to several hundred dollars. For ticket information, contact the **FedEx Forum box office** (191 Beale St., 901/205-2640, www.fedexforum.com, Mon.–Fri. 10 A.M.–5:30 P.M.). The NBA season runs October–April.

The **University of Memphis Tigers** surprised many in 2008 by making it all the way to the NCAA Championship. The team's remarkable 38–2 season brought new energy and excitement to the university's basketball program.

You can watch Tigers basketball November–April at FedEx Forum. Tickets are available from the FedEx Forum box office, or contact University of Memphis Athletics (www.gotigersgo.com) for more information.

Baseball

From April to October, the **Memphis Redbirds** (901/721-6000, www.memphisredbirds.com, $6–26) play AAA ball at the striking **AutoZone Park** in downtown Memphis. The stadium is bounded by Union Avenue, Madison Avenue, and 3rd Street, and is convenient to dozens of downtown hotels and restaurants. The Redbirds are an affiliate of the St. Louis Cardinals. Cheap tickets ($6) buy you a seat on the grassy berm, or you can pay a little more for seats in the stadium or boxes.

The Redbirds are owned by a nonprofit organization that also operates a number of community and youth programs in the city.

Racing

The **Memphis International Raceway** (550 Victory Ln., 901/969-7223, www.racemir.com) is located a short drive from downtown Memphis in Millington, northeast of the city center. The park includes a 0.75-mile

© ANDREA ZUCKER/MEMPHIS VISITORS BUREAU

Root, root, root for the Redbirds at AutoZone Park.

NASCAR oval, a 0.25-mile drag racing strip, and a 1.77-mile road course. It hosts more than 200 race events every year, including a stop in the annual Busch Series races.

Millington is located about 30 minutes' drive north of Memphis.

Ice Hockey

The **Riverkings** (662/342-1755, www.riverkings.com, $16–27) play minor-league ice hockey at the **DeSoto Civic Center** (4650 Venture Dr., Southaven, MS), about 20 miles south of Memphis.

Accommodations

There are thousands of cookie-cutter hotel rooms in Memphis, but travelers would be wise to look past major chains. If you can afford it, choose to stay in downtown Memphis. With the city at your doorstep, you'll have a better experience both day and night. Downtown is also where you'll find the most distinctive accommodations, including fine luxury hotels, charming inns, and an antebellum guest home.

Budget travelers have their pick of major chain hotels; the farther from the city center, the cheaper the room. Beware very good deals, however, since you may find yourself in sketchy neighborhoods. There is a campground with tent and RV sites within a 15-minute drive of downtown at T. O. Fuller State Park.

DOWNTOWN
$150-200

The ⟨ **Talbot Heirs Guesthouse** (99 S. 2nd St., 901/527-9772, www.talbotheirs.com, $130–275), in the heart of downtown, offers a winning balance of comfort and sophistication. Each of the inn's nine rooms has its own unique decor—from cheerful red walls to black-and-white chic. All rooms are thoughtfully outfitted with a full kitchen and modern bathroom, television, radio and CD player, sitting area, desk, and high-speed Internet. Little extras like the refrigerator stocked for breakfast go a long way, as does the cheerful yet efficient welcome provided by proprietors Tom and Sandy Franck. Book early since the Talbot Heirs is often full, especially during peak summer months.

Over $200

In 2007, Memphis welcomed the **Westin Memphis Beale Street** (170 George W. Lee Ave., 901/334-5900, $199–369), located across the street from FedEx Forum and one block from Beale Street. The hotel's 203 guest rooms are plush and modern, each with a work desk, high-speed Internet, MP3-player docking station, and super-comfortable beds. The location can be noisy when Beale Street is in full swing.

The **Hampton Inn & Suites** (175 Peabody Pl., 901/260-4000, www.bealestreetsuites.hamptoninn.com, $199–275) is less than a block from Beale Street. The Hampton has 144 standard rooms with high-speed Internet and standard hotel accommodations. The 30 suites ($250) have kitchens and separate living quarters. The entire hotel is nonsmoking.

Plans were afoot for a Hyatt Regency hotel at One Beale (www.onebeale.2dimes.com), a $175 million mixed-use development that would sit on the riverfront at the head of Beale Street. The stalled economy put things on hold. If condo sales and other financing come through, then this may be Memphis's most luxurious hotel.

UPTOWN
$100-150

The most affordable downtown accommodations are in chain hotels. One of the best choices is the **Sleep Inn at Court Square** (40 N. Front St., 901/522-9700, $119–299), with 124 simple but clean and well-maintained rooms. Guests have access to a small fitness room, free parking, and a free continental breakfast. For those with a bigger appetite, the excellent Blue Plate Café is just across the square. It's a five-block walk to Beale Street from Court Square, but the trolley runs right past the front door of the hotel.

Even closer to the action is the 71-room **Comfort Inn Downtown** (100 N. Front St., 901/526-0583, $119–149). This hotel is within easy walking distance of all the city-center attractions. Rooms aren't anything special, but the staff are often quite friendly; guests get free breakfast, Internet access, and indoor parking; and there's an outdoor pool. Ask for a room facing west, and you'll have a nice view of the Mississippi River. Parking is $8.

$150-200

Near AutoZone Park and a lot of restaurants is **Doubletree Downtown Memphis** (185 Union Ave., 901/528-1800, $134–299). A 272-room hotel set in the restored Tennessee Hotel, the Doubletree maintains a touch of the old grandeur of the 1929 hotel from which it was crafted. Rooms are large, and there's an outdoor swimming pool and fitness room. Valet parking is $22 or more per night.

If you want to be in the middle of things but can't afford to stay at the swanky Peabody, consider the **Holiday Inn Select** (160 Union Ave., 901/525-5491, www.hisdowntownmemphis.com, $139–199). Located across the street from the Peabody and near AutoZone Park, this Holiday Inn routinely gets good reviews from travelers.

Over $200

C The Peabody Memphis (149 Union Ave., 901/529-4000 or 800/732-2639, www.peabodymemphis.com, $230–2,500 for a presidential suite) is the city's signature hotel. Founded in 1869, the Peabody was the grand hotel of the South, and the hotel has preserved some of its traditional Southern charm. Tuxedoed bellhops greet you at the door, and all guests

receive a complimentary shoeshine. Rooms are nicely appointed with plantation-style furniture, free wireless Internet, and in-room safes, as well as all the amenities typical of an upper-tier hotel. Several fine restaurants are located on the ground floor, including the lobby bar, which is the gathering place for the twice-daily red carpet march of the famous Peabody ducks.

One of Memphis's newer hotels is the **River Inn of Harbor Town** (50 Harbor Town Sq., 901/260-3333, www.riverinnmemphis.com, $176–599). A 28-room boutique hotel on Mud Island, the River Inn offers great river views and a unique location that is just minutes from downtown. Set in the mixed residential and commercial New Urban community of Harbor Town, the River Inn provides guests with super amenities like a fitness center, reading rooms, free wireless Internet, free parking, modern decor and furniture, two restaurants, a 1.5-mile walking trail, and spa. Even the most modest rooms have luxurious extras like 32-inch flat-screen televisions, chocolate truffle turndown service, and full gourmet breakfast at Currents, one of two restaurants on the property. The River Inn offers the best of both worlds—a relaxing and quiet getaway that is uniquely convenient to the center of Memphis.

Seeking to be the finest hotel in Memphis, the **Madison Hotel** (79 Madison Ave., 901/333-1200, www.madisonhotelmemphis.com, $200–2,500) is appropriately upscale. The decor is modern, with a touch of art deco. Guests enjoy every perk you can imagine, from valet parking to room service from one of the city's finest restaurants, Grill 83. The daily continental breakfast and afternoon happy hour are an opportunity to enjoy the view from the top floor of the old bank building that houses the hotel. The 110 rooms have wet bars, Internet access, and luxurious bathrooms.

MIDTOWN

Midtown hotels are cheaper than those in downtown. If you have a car, they are convenient to city-center attractions as well as those in midtown itself.

Under $100

There are a few budget hotels within trolley distance of downtown. The **Union Express** (42 S. Camilla St., 901/526-1050, $60–80) is about two blocks from the Madison Avenue trolley and has a dismal, but free, breakfast. The **Motel 6** (210 S. Pauline St., 901/528-0650, $45–59) is about three blocks from the trolley. These choices are certainly not ritzy, but they're acceptable and welcome a large number of budget travelers.

$100-150

The **Best Western Gen X Inn** (1177 Madison Ave., 901/692-9136, $89–180) straddles downtown and midtown Memphis. Located about two miles from the city center along the Madison Avenue trolley line, Gen Xers can get downtown on the trolley in about 15 minutes with a little luck. The hotel, which has free parking and breakfast, is also accessible to the city's expansive medical center and the attractions around Overton Park. These rooms are standard hotel style, enhanced with bright colors, flat-panel plasma TVs, and a general aura of youthfulness. The whole hotel is non-smoking, and guests enjoy a good continental breakfast and a special partnership with the downtown YMCA for gym use. This is a good choice for travelers who want to be near downtown but are on a budget, particularly those with a car. No pets are permitted here.

$150-200

If you want to cook some of your own meals and have comforts like on-site laundry facilities, **Shellcrest** (669 Jefferson Ave., 901/277-0223, www.shellcrest.com, $175 per night, $1,700 per month) is a good choice. This handsome redbrick town house is about six blocks east of downtown. It is designed to be an extended-stay hotel—most leases are for at least

one month. But if they have a vacancy and you are looking to stay for at least three nights, the owners will accommodate short-term guests at a rate of $175 per night. You get a lot for your money: The accommodations are in spacious one-bedroom apartments with a parlor, sunroom, and study, as well as a gourmet kitchen where you can cook your own meals.

The **Holiday Inn-University of Memphis** (3700 Central Ave., 901/678-8200, $119–160) is part of the university's hospitality school. All rooms are suites, with a wet bar and microwave, sitting room, and spacious bathrooms. The lobby contains an exhibit on Kemmons Wilson, the Memphis-born founder of Holiday Inn, who is credited with inventing the modern hotel industry. It is located about six miles from downtown Memphis.

Over $200

You can sleep where Elvis slept at **C Lauderdale Courts** (185 Winchester, 901/523-8662, www.lauderdalecourts.com, $250). The onetime housing project where Elvis and his parents lived after they moved to Memphis from Mississippi is now a neat midtown apartment complex. The rooms where the Presleys lived have been restored to their 1950s greatness, and guests can use the working 1951 Frigidaire. The rooms are decorated with Presley family photographs and other Elvis memorabilia. You can rent Lauderdale Courts No. 328 for up to six nights. It sleeps up to four adults. The rooms are not rented during Elvis Week in August or his birthday week in January, when the suite is open for public viewing for $10 per person.

SOUTH MEMPHIS

There are two reasons to stay in south Memphis: the airport and Graceland. But even if you are keenly interested in either of these places, you should think twice about staying in this part of town. You will need a car, as some

Affordable doesn't mean lackluster at the Clarion Memphis Airport/Graceland hotel.

of these neighborhoods are seedy. A car is also a must as south Memphis is not in walking distance of anything of interest.

Under $100

If you need a place to stay near the airport, you can't get any closer than the **Regency Inn & Suites Memphis Airport** (2411 Winchester Rd., 901/332-2370, $69–109), which is right next door. In addition to offering a pool and fitness center, this hotel will shuttle you to the airport terminal for free. Another airport option is the **Memphis Airport Hotel & Conference Center** (2240 Democrat Rd., 901/332-1130, $80–130), which caters to business travelers. There is a guest laundry, free airport shuttle, room service, business center, and good fitness room.

You can't sleep much closer to Graceland than the **Days Inn at Graceland** (3839 Elvis Presley Blvd., 901/346-5500, $70–110), one of the most well-worn properties in the venerable Days Inn chain. The hotel has amped up the Elvis kitsch; you can tune into free nonstop Elvis movies or swim in a guitar-shaped pool. There is a free continental breakfast. Book early for Elvis Week.

The totally renovated **Clarion Memphis Airport/Graceland** (1471 E. Brooks Rd., 901/332-3500, www.cedarstreethospitality. com/thecedarhotel.php, $89–124) is now a tidy, safe oasis in an otherwise unappealing part of town. Before its remodel, being close to Graceland and the airport were the only draws of this budget hotel. It remains affordable, but now it has the added perk of being clean, with updated rooms and bathrooms, plus a new restaurant and bar. There's a nice outdoor pool, a small fitness room, and a lovely lobby. Book early for Elvis Week.

$100-150

For the most Elvis-y Graceland digs, why not give in and stay at the **Elvis Presley Heartbreak Hotel** (3677 Elvis Presley Blvd.,

901/332-1000, www.heartbreakhotel.net, $115–153)? This 128-room hotel has special Elvis-themed suites ($555–601), and the lobby and common areas have a special Elvis flair. Elvis enthusiasts should check out special package deals with the hotel and Graceland.

CAMPING

You can pitch your tent or park your RV just 15 minutes' drive from downtown Memphis at **T. O. Fuller State Park** (1500 Mitchell Rd., 901/543-7581). The park has 45 tent and RV sites, each with a picnic table, fire ring, grill, lantern hanger, and electrical and water hookups. Sites are allocated on a first-come,

first-served basis; reservations are not accepted. Rates are $20 a night per site.

On the north side of Memphis, **Meeman-Shelby Forest State Park** (910 Riddick Rd., Millington, 901/876-5215) is a half-hour drive from downtown. Stay in one of six lakeside cabins, which you can reserve up to one year in advance; book at least one month in advance to avoid being shut out. The two-bedroom cabins can sleep up to six people. Rates are $80–100 per night, depending on the season and day of the week. There are also 49 tent/RV sites, each with electrical and water hookups, picnic tables, grills, and fire rings. The bathhouse has hot showers. Campsite rates are $20 per night.

Food

Eating may be the best thing about visiting Memphis. The city's culinary specialties start—but don't end—with barbecue. Plate-lunch diners around the city offer delectable corn bread, fried chicken, greens, fried green tomatoes, peach cobbler, and dozens of other Southern specialties on a daily basis. And to make it even better, such down-home restaurants are easy on your wallet. For those seeking a departure from home-style fare, Memphis has dozens of fine restaurants, some old established eateries and others newcomers that are as trendy as those in any major American city.

CAFÉS AND DINERS
Downtown

You can order deli sandwiches, breakfast plates, and a limited variety of plate lunches at the **Front Street Deli** (77 S. Front St., 901/522-8943, Mon.–Fri. 7 A.M.–2 P.M., $4–9). The deli, which claims to be Memphis's oldest, serves breakfast and lunch on weekdays only. One of its claims to fame is that scenes from *The Firm* were filmed here.

For the best burgers on Beale Street, go to

Dyers (205 Beale St., 901/527-3937, www.dyersonbeale.com, Sun.–Thurs. 11 A.M.–1 A.M., Fri.–Sat. 11 A.M.–5 A.M., $7–12). The legend is that Dyers's secret is that it has been using the same grease (strained daily) since it opened in 1912. Only in Tennessee could century-old grease be a selling point. True or not, the burgers here are especially juicy. Dyers also serves wings, hot dogs, milk shakes, and a full array of fried sides.

For coffee, pastries, and fruit smoothies, **Bluff City Coffee** (505 S. Main St., 901/405-4399, www.bluffcitycoffee.com, Mon.–Sat. 6:30 A.M.–6 P.M., Sun. 8 A.M.–6 P.M., $2–5) is your best bet in this part of the city. Located in the South Main district of galleries and condos, the shop is decorated with large prints of vintage Memphis photographs, and it is also a wireless Internet hot spot.

Midtown

No restaurant has a larger or more loyal following in midtown than **Young Avenue Deli** (2119 Young Ave., 901/278-0034, www.younggavenuedeli.com, Mon.–Sat. 11 A.M.–3 A.M., Sun. noon–3 A.M., $4–8), which serves a dozen different specialty sandwiches, grill fare including burgers and chicken sandwiches, plus salads and sides. The Bren—smoked turkey, mushrooms, onions, and cream cheese in a steamed pita—is a deli favorite. The food is certainly good, but it's the atmosphere at this homey yet hip Cooper-Young institution that really pulls in the crowds. There is live music most weekends, and the bar serves a kaleidoscope of domestic and imported beer, including lots of hard-to-find microbrews. The deli serves lunch and dinner daily.

For a good cup of coffee in the Cooper-Young neighborhood, head to **Java Cabana** (2170 Young Ave., 901/272-7210, www.javacabanacoffeehouse.com, Tues.–Thurs. 6:30 A.M.–10 P.M., Fri.–Sat. 9 A.M.–midnight, Sun. noon–10 P.M., $4–10). Java Cabana serves light breakfast fare, including pancakes and omelets, all day. For lunch or later, you can order simple sandwiches or munchies like apple slices and peanut butter, potato chips, or Pop Tarts.

For a cold treat during the long, hot Memphis summer, head to **Wiles-Smith Drug Store** (1635 Union Ave., 901/278-6416, Mon.–Wed. 9 A.M.–5 P.M., Thurs. 9 A.M.–2 P.M., Sat. 10 A.M.–3 P.M.) for a milk shake. The lunch counter at this old-fashioned drugstore also serves sandwiches and snacks, but it is the milk shakes that draw the biggest crowd. They come in chocolate, vanilla, strawberry, and cherry, and customers get to pour the cool, frothy treat into their own glass.

SOUTHERN
Downtown
Tucked inside an unassuming storefront across from the valet entrance to the Peabody Hotel is **Flying Fish** (105 S. 2nd St., 901/522-8228, daily 11 A.M.–10 P.M., $5–14), your first stop for authentic fried catfish in Memphis. If catfish isn't your thing, try the grilled or boiled shrimp, fish tacos, frog legs, or oysters. The baskets of fried seafood come with fries and hush puppies, and the grilled plates come with grilled veggies, rice, and beans. The tangy coleslaw is a must. The atmosphere here is laid-back; place your order at the window and come and get it when the coaster they give you starts to vibrate. The checkered tables are well stocked with hot sauce and saltines.

It would be a grave mistake to visit Memphis and not stop at ◖ **Gus's World Famous Fried Chicken** (310 Front St., 901/527-4877, Mon.–Thurs. and Sun. 11 A.M.–9 P.M., Fri.–Sat. 11 A.M.–10:30 P.M., $6–12) for some of their delicious fried bird. The downtown location is a franchise of the original Gus's, which is a half-hour drive northeast out of town along U.S. 70, in Mason. It is no exaggeration to say that Gus's cooks up some of the best fried chicken out there: It is spicy, juicy, and hot. It's served casually wrapped in brown paper. Sides include coleslaw, baked beans, and fried pickles. They also serve grilled-cheese sandwiches. The service in this hole-in-the-wall establishment is slow but friendly, so come in with a smile on.

The **Arcade** (540 S. Main St., 901/526-5757, www.arcaderestaurant.com, daily 7 A.M.–3 P.M., $5–10) is said to be Memphis's oldest restaurant. Founded in 1919 and still operated by the same family (with lots of the same decor), this restaurant feels like a throwback to an earlier time. The menu is diverse, with pizzas, sandwiches, plate-lunch specials during the week, and breakfast served anytime. The chicken spaghetti is a stick-to-your-ribs favorite.

Uptown
◖ **The Little Tea Shop** (69 Monroe, 901/525-6000, Mon.–Fri. 11 A.M.–2 P.M., $4.95–7.50) serves traditional plate lunches through the week. Choose from daily specials like fried catfish, chicken potpie, and meat loaf with your choice of vegetable and side dishes by ticking off check boxes on the menu. Every meal (except sandwiches) comes with fresh, hot corn bread that might well be the star of the show.

This is stick-to-your-ribs Southern cooking at its best, so come hungry. If you have room, try the peach cobbler or pecan ball for dessert. The staff's welcoming yet efficient style makes this perfect for a quick lunch. Not to be missed.

The Blue Plate Cafe (113 Court Square S., 901/523-2050, Mon.–Sat. 6 A.M.–8:30 P.M., $4–10) serves hearty breakfasts, plate lunches, and traditional home-style cooking. Its newsprint menu imparts wisdom ("Rule of Life No. 1: Wake up. Show up. Pay attention.") and declares that every day should begin with a great breakfast. It's not hard to comply at the Blue Plate. Eggs come with homemade biscuits and gravy, and your choice of grits, hash browns, or pancakes. For lunch, try a meat-and-three or vegetable plate, slow-cooked white-bean soup, or a grilled peanut butter and banana sandwich. Locals swear by the fried green tomatoes. There are three Blue Plate Cafes in Memphis; the other two are at 2921 Kirby Whitten Road in Bartlett (901/213-1066) and at 5469 Poplar Avenue in an old house in midtown (901/761-9696).

Alcenia's (317 N. Main St., 901/523-0200, www.alcenias.com, Tues.–Fri. 11 A.M.–5 P.M., Sat. 9 A.M.–3 P.M., $4–10), located in the Pinch district, is among Memphis's best Southern-style restaurants. Known for its plate lunches, fried chicken, and pastries, Alcenia's has a style unlike any other Memphis eatery, witnessed in its offbeat decor of '60s-style beads, folk art, and wedding lace. Proprietor B. J. Chester-Tamayo is all love, and she pours her devotion into some of the city's best soul food. Try the spicy cabbage and deep-fried chicken, and save room for Alcenia's famous bread pudding for dessert. Chicken and waffles is the Saturday-morning specialty.

Midtown

Just follow the crowds to the **Cupboard Restaurant** (1400 Union Ave., 901/276-8015, daily 7 A.M.–8 P.M., $6–9), one of Memphians'

favorite stops for plate lunches. The Cupboard moved from its downtown location to an old Shoney's about a mile outside of town to accommodate the throngs who stop here for authentic home-style cooking. The Cupboard gets only the freshest vegetables for its dishes like okra and tomatoes, rutabaga turnips, steamed cabbage, and green beans. The meat specials change daily but include things like fried chicken, chicken and dumplings, hamburger steak with onions, and beef tips with noodles. The corn bread "coins" are exceptionally buttery, and the bread is baked fresh daily. For dessert, try the lemon icebox pie.

The Women's Exchange Tea Room (88 Racine St., 901/327-5681, www.womans-exchange.com, Mon.–Fri. 11:30 A.M.–1:45 P.M., $10) feels like a throwback to an earlier era. Located one block east of the Poplar Street viaduct, the Women's Exchange has been serving lunch since 1936, and the menu has not changed much over the years. The special changes daily and always includes a choice of two entrées, or a four-vegetable plate. Classics like chicken salad, salmon loaf, beef tenderloin, and seafood gumbo are favorites, and all lunches come with a drink and dessert. The dining room looks out onto a green garden, and the atmosphere is homey—not stuffy. The Exchange also sells gifts, housewares, and other knickknacks.

In the Cooper-Young neighborhood, **Soul Fish** (862 S. Cooper St., 901/725-0722, Mon.–Sat. 11 A.M.–10 P.M., Sun. 11 A.M.–9 P.M., $6–15) offers traditional plate lunches, vegetable plates, and several varieties of catfish. You can get the fish breaded and fried, or blackened with a potent spice mix. Soul Fish is owned in part by Tiger Bryant, owner of the venerable Young Avenue Deli, and it has the hallmarks of a well-conceived eatery. The atmosphere is open and cheerful, with a few touches of subtle sophistication. In this case, the main attraction is good food at a good price—a combination that can be hard to find elsewhere in Cooper-Young.

South Memphis

Gay Hawk Restaurant (685 Danny Thomas

Blvd., 901/947-1464, Mon.–Fri. 11 A.M.–3 P.M., Sat.–Sun. noon–5 P.M., $6–10) serves country-style food that sticks to your ribs and warms your soul. Chef Bobo declares that his specialty is "home-cooked food," and it really is as simple as that. The best thing about Gay Hawk is the luncheon buffet, which lets newcomers to Southern cooking survey the choices and try a little bit of everything. The Sunday lunch buffet practically sags with specialties like fried chicken, grilled fish, macaroni and cheese, greens, and much, much more. Save room for peach cobbler.

❿ BARBECUE

Barbecue is serious business in Memphis, unlike anywhere else in the state. On the northern fringe of downtown Memphis is one of the city's most famous and well-loved barbecue joints: **❿ Cozy Corner** (745 N. Parkway, 901/527-9158, www.cozycornerbbq.com, Tues.–Sat. 11 A.M.–9 P.M., $4–16). Cozy Corner is tucked into a storefront in an otherwise abandoned strip mall; you'll smell it before you see it. Step inside to order barbecue pork, sausage, or bologna sandwiches. Or get a two-bone, four-bone, or six-bone rib dinner plate, which comes with your choice of baked beans, coleslaw, or barbecue spaghetti, plus slices of Wonder bread to sop up the juices. One of Cozy Corner's specialties is its barbecued Cornish hens—a preparation that is surprising but delicious. Sweet tea goes perfectly with the tangy and spicy barbecue.

Jim Neely's **Interstate Bar-B-Que** (2265 S. 3rd St., 901/775-2304, www.interstatebarbecue.com, Mon.–Thurs. 11 A.M.–11 P.M., Fri.–Sat. 11 A.M.–midnight, $5–18) was once ranked the second-best barbecue in the nation, but the proprietors have not let it go to their heads; this is still a down-to-earth, no-frills eatery. Large appetites can order a whole slab of pork or beef ribs, but most people will be satisfied with a chopped pork sandwich, which comes topped with coleslaw and smothered with barbecue

sauce. Families can get the fixings for 6, 8, or 10 sandwiches sent out family style. For an adventure, try the barbecue spaghetti or barbecue bologna sandwich. If you're in a hurry, the Interstate has a drive-up window, too, and if you are really smitten, you can order pork, sauce, and seasoning in bulk to be frozen and shipped to your home.

Although aficionados will remind you that the ribs served at the **Rendezvous** (52 S. 2nd St., 901/523-2746, www.hogsfly.com, Tues.–Thurs. 4:30–10:30 P.M., Fri. 11 A.M.–11 P.M., Sat. 11:30 A.M.–11 P.M., $8–16) are not technically barbecue, they are one of the biggest barbecue stories in town. Covered in a dry rub of spices and broiled until the meat falls off the bones, these ribs will knock your socks off. If you prefer, you can choose Charlie Vergos's dry-rub chicken or boneless pork loin. Orders come with baked beans and coleslaw, but beer is really the essential accompaniment to any Vergos meal. The door to Rendezvous is tucked in an alley off Monroe Avenue. The smoky interior, decorated with antiques and yellowing business cards, is low-key, noisy, and lots of fun.

A Memphis chain, **Gridley's** (6842 Stage Rd., 901/377-8055, Mon. and Wed.–Fri. 11 A.M.–8 P.M., Sat. 11 A.M.–9 P.M., $4–18) serves wet-style barbecue ribs, pork shoulder plates and sandwiches, plus spicy grilled shrimp. The shrimp is served with a buttery and delicious dipping sauce. Try the half pork, half shrimp plate for a real treat. Meals here come with baked beans, slaw, and hot fresh bread.

CONTEMPORARY
Downtown

The Majestic Grill (145 S. Main St., 901/522-8555, www.majesticgrille.com, Mon.–Thurs. 11 A.M.–10 P.M., Fri.–Sat. 11 A.M.–11 P.M., Sun. 11 A.M.–9 P.M., $6–34) serves a remarkably affordable yet upscale menu at lunch and dinner. Located in what was once the Majestic Theater, the restaurant's white tablecloths and apron-clad waiters lend an aura of refinement. But with main courses starting at just $6, this can be a bargain. Flatbread pizzas feature asparagus, spicy shrimp, and smoked sausage, and sandwiches include burgers and clubs. Specialties include pasta, barbecue ribs, grilled salmon, and steaks. Don't pass on dessert, served in individual shot glasses, such as chocolate mousse, key lime pie, and carrot cake, among others.

It is impossible to pigeonhole **Automatic Slim's Tonga Club** (83 S. 2nd St., 901/525-7948, Mon.–Fri. 11 A.M.–midnight, Sat.–Sun. 10 A.M.–10 P.M., $12–20), except to say that this Memphis institution consistently offers fresh, spirited, and original fare. Named after a character from an old blues tune, Automatic Slim's uses lots of strong flavors to create its eclectic menu; Caribbean and Southwestern influences are the most apparent. Take a seat, and in two shakes you'll be presented with soft, fresh bread and pesto-seasoned olive oil for dipping. The Caribbean shrimp are a favorite of many diners. A meal at Automatic Slim's would not be complete without a famous Tonga Martini or one of the kitchen's delectable desserts: Pecan tart and chocolate cake are good choices. Automatic Slim's is a welcome departure from barbecue and Southern food when you're ready. Its atmosphere is relaxed, and there's often a crowd at the bar, especially on weekends when there's live music on tap.

Long the standard-bearer of fine French cuisine, **Chez Philippe** (149 Union Ave., 901/529-4000, Wed.–Sat. 6–10 P.M., afternoon tea Wed.–Sun., $78–100), located in the Peabody Hotel, now offers French-Asian fusion cuisine. The Asian influences are noticeable in the ingredients, but the preparation of most dishes at Chez Philippe remains traditional French. Entrées include grouper, bass, pork chop, and venison. Chez Philippe offers a prix fixe menu: Three courses is $78, and five courses is $88. Or opt for a seven-course tasting menu for $100; wine pairings are an additional $48 per person.

Midtown

In 2007, Memphis's foremost restaurateur, Karen Blockman Carrier, closed her fine-dining restaurant Cielo in Victorian Village, redecorated, and reopened it as the **Molly Fontaine Lounge** (679 Adams Ave., 901/524-1886, Wed.–Sat. 5 P.M.–2:30 A.M., $12–24). Carrier's vision was an old-fashioned club where guests can order upscale cocktails, relax with live music, and eat tasty Mediterranean- and Middle Eastern–inspired tapas. The restaurant has an upmarket but cozy atmosphere, with equal measures of funky and fine. The live piano jazz is the perfect backdrop for the restaurant's artistic small plates.

Surprisingly good for a bookstore café, **Bronte** (387 Perkins Ext., 901/374-0881, Mon.–Thurs. 8 A.M.–9 P.M., Fri.–Sat. 8 A.M.–10 P.M., Sun. 9 A.M.–8 P.M., $8–12), inside Davis-Kidd Booksellers, offers salads, soups, and sandwiches, as well as daily meat and fish specials. The soup-and-sandwich combo is filling and good. Breakfast may well be the best meal on offer, however. The morning menu features specials designed by celebrity chefs, including omelets, baked goods, and crepes.

One of Memphis's most distinctive restaurant settings is an old beauty shop in the Cooper-Young neighborhood. **◖ The Beauty Shop** (966 S. Cooper St., 901/272-7111, www.thebeautyshoprestaurant.com, Mon.–Sat. 11 A.M.–2 P.M., Mon.–Thurs. 5–10 P.M., Fri.–Sat. 5–11 P.M., Sun. 10 A.M.–3 P.M., $8–32) takes advantage of the vintage beauty parlor decor to create a great talking point for patrons and food writers alike. The domed hair dryers remain, and the restaurant has put the shampooing sinks to work as beer coolers. At lunch, the Beauty Shop offers a casual menu of sandwiches and salads. For dinner, the imaginative cuisine of Memphis restaurateur Karen Blockman Carrier, who also owns Molly Fontaine Lounge and Automatic Slim's Tonga Club, takes over.

At The Beauty Shop in the Cooper-Young neighborhood, you'll dine in an old – you guessed it – beauty parlor.

Right next to the Beauty Shop is **Do** (964 S. Cooper St., 901/272-0830, Mon.–Thurs. 5–10 P.M., Fri.–Sat. 5–11 P.M., Sun. 5–9 P.M., $6–15), a trendy sushi restaurant that also offers tempura, soups, and salads.

If you enjoy your beer as much or more than your meal, then head straight for **Boscos Squared** (2120 Madison Ave., 901/432-2222, www.boscosbeer.com, Mon.–Thurs. 11 A.M.–2 A.M., Fri.–Sat. 11 A.M.–3 A.M., Sun. 10:30 A.M.–2 A.M., $12–22). Boscos is a brewpub with fresh seafood, steak, and pizza. Their beer menu is among the best in the city, and many of the brews are made on the premises. Boscos also has locations in Franklin and Nashville.

East Memphis

To many minds, Memphis dining gets no better than **Erling Jensen, The Restaurant** (1044 S. Yates Rd., 901/763-3700, www. ejensen.com, daily 5–10 P.M., $30–50).

Danish-born Erling Jensen is the mastermind of this fine-dining restaurant that has consistently earned marks as Memphians' favorite restaurant. Understated decor and friendly service are the backdrop to Jensen's dishes, which are works of art. The menu changes with the seasons and based upon availability, but usually it includes about six different seafood dishes and as many meat and game choices. Black Angus beef, elk loin, and buffalo tenderloin are some of the favorites. Meals at Jensen's restaurant should begin with an appetizer, salad, or soup—or all three. The jumbo chunk crab cakes with smoked red-pepper sauce are excellent. Reservations are a good idea at Erling Jensen, and so are jackets for men. Expect to spend upwards of $80 for a four-course meal here; $60 for two courses. Add more for wine.

Memphis's premier steak house is **Folk's Folly** (551 S. Mendenhall Rd.,

PIGGLY WIGGLY

Memphian Clarence Saunders opened the first Piggly Wiggly at 79 Jefferson Street in 1916, thus giving birth to the modern American supermarket. Until then, shoppers went to small storefront shops where they would ask the counter clerk for what they needed: a pound of flour, a half dozen pickles, a block of cheese. The clerk went to the bulk storage area at the rear of the store and measured out what the customer needed.

Saunders's big idea was self-service. At the Piggly Wiggly, customers entered the store, carried a basket, and were able to pick out prepackaged and priced containers of food, which they paid for at the payment station on their way out.

Suffice to say, the Piggly Wiggly idea took off, and by 1923 there were 1,268 Piggly Wiggly franchises around the country. Saunders used some of his profits to build a massive mansion east of the city out of pink Georgia limestone, but he was never to live in the Pink Palace, which he lost as a result of a complex stock loss.

Today, Saunders's Pink Palace is home to the Pink Palace Museum, which includes, among other things, a replica of the original Piggly Wiggly supermarket.

901/762-8200, www.folksfolly.com, Mon.–Sat. 5:30–10 P.M., Sun. 5:30–9 P.M., $30–70), located just east of Audubon Park. Diners flock here for prime aged steaks and seafood favorites. For small appetites, try the 8-ounce filet mignon for $32; large appetites can gorge on the 28-ounce porterhouse for $60. Seafood includes lobster, crab legs, and wild salmon. The atmosphere is classic steak house: The lighting is low, and there's a piano bar on the property.

Some say **Acre Restaurant** (690 S. Perkins, 901/818-2273, www.acrememphis.com, Mon.–Fri. 11 A.M.–2 P.M.,

Mon.–Sat. 5–10 P.M., $25–80) is Memphis's best. Certainly, it has one of the best wine lists in town. The menu combines Southern and Asian traditions with locally grown and raised ingredients in a modern setting.

Where else in the world can you enjoy the offbeat combination that is **Jerry's Sno-Cone and Car Wash** (1657 Wells Station Rd., 901/767-2659, Mon.–Sat. 11 A.M.–7 P.M.)?

INTERNATIONAL
Downtown

For sushi, try **Sekisui** (Union at 2nd Ave., 901/523-0001, www.sekisuiusa.com, Mon.–Sun. noon–3 P.M. and 6–11 P.M.), where a roll costs $2.50–8, and a filling combo plate will run you about $15. The downtown restaurant is located on the ground floor of the Holiday Inn Select. Sekisui is a Memphis chain, and there are other locations in midtown and the suburbs, as well as in Chattanooga.

Midtown

The **India Palace** (1720 Poplar Ave., 901/278-1199, www.indiapalaceinc.com, daily 11 A.M.–3 P.M. and 5–10 P.M., $7–17) is a regular winner in reader's choice polls for Indian food in Memphis. The lunchtime buffet is filling and economical, and the dinner menu features vegetarian, chicken, and seafood dishes. The dinner platters are generous and tasty.

Pho Hoa Binh (1615 Madison, 901/276-0006, Mon.–Fri. 11 A.M.–9 P.M., Sat. noon–9 P.M., $4–9) is one of the most popular Vietnamese restaurants in town. You can't beat the value of the lunch buffet, or you can order from the dizzying array of Chinese and Vietnamese dishes, including spring rolls, vermicelli noodle bowls, rice, and meat dishes. There are a lot of vegetarian options here.

The atmosphere at **Bhan Thai** (1324 Peabody Ave., 901/272-1538, www.bhanthairestaurant.com, Tues.–Fri. 11 A.M.–2:30 P.M., Sun.–Thurs. 5–9:30 P.M., Fri.–Sat. 5–10:30 P.M., $10–19) in midtown is almost as appealing as the excellent Thai food served there. Set in an elegant 1912 home, Bhan Thai makes the most of the house's space, and seating is spread throughout several colorful rooms and on the back patio. Choose from dishes like red snapper, masaman curry, and roasted duck curry. The Bhan Thai salad is popular, with creamy peanut dressing and crisp vegetables.

It's the regulars who are happy at the **Happy Mexican Restaurant and Cantina** (385 S. 2nd St., 901/529-9991, www.happymexican. com, Sun.–Thurs. 11 A.M.–10 P.M., Fri.–Sat. 11 A.M.–11 P.M., $7–15). Serving generous portions of homemade Mexican food for lunch and dinner, Happy Mexican is destined to become a downtown favorite. The service is efficient and friendly, and the decor is cheerful but not over the top. It's located just a few blocks south of the National Civil Rights Museum. There are three other locations in the greater Memphis area.

MARKETS

The only downtown grocery store is the **Easy-Way** (80 N. Main St., 901/523-1323, Mon.–Sat. 7 A.M.–6 P.M.), on the corner of Main Street and Jefferson Avenue. For liquor and wine, go to **The Corkscrew** (511 S. Front St., 901/523-9389).

The closest gourmet grocery is located in Harbor Town, the residential community on Mud Island, where **Miss Cordelia's** (737 Harbor Bend, 901/526-4772, www.misscordelias.com, daily 7 A.M.–10 P.M.) sells fresh produce, bakery goods, and staples. A deli in the back serves soups, salads, sandwiches, and a wide variety of prepared foods.

For a full-service grocery store in midtown, look for the **Kroger** at the corner of Cleveland and Poplar.

The **Memphis Farmer's Market** (901/575-0580, www.memphisfarmersmarket.com, Apr.–Oct. Sat. 7 A.M.–1 P.M., rain or shine) takes place in the pavilion opposite Central Station in the South Main part of town.

Information and Services

INFORMATION
Visitors Centers
The city's visitors center is the **Tennessee Welcome Center** (119 Riverside Dr., 901/543-6757), located on the Tennessee side of the I-40 bridge. The center has lots of brochures and free maps and staff who can answer your questions. It is open 24 hours a day, seven days a week. The center assists more than 350,000 travelers annually.

Although it is not designed to be a visitors center per se, the **Memphis Convention and Visitors Bureau** (47 Union Ave., 901/543-5300, www.memphistravel.com, Apr.–Sept. daily 9 A.M.–6 P.M., Oct.–Mar. Mon.–Fri 9 A.M.–5 P.M.) is a resource for visitors. You can collect maps and ask questions here. The bureau also produces videos highlighting city

attractions and restaurants, which are available on many hotel televisions.

Maps
Hand-out maps that highlight key attractions are available from visitors centers in Memphis. If you are only interested in Beale Street, Graceland, and the interstates, these will be fine. The free maps provided at the concierge desk of the Peabody Hotel are particularly well marked and useful.

If you want to explore further, or if you plan to drive yourself around the city, it is wise to get a proper city map or GPS. Rand McNally publishes a detailed Memphis city map, which you can buy from bookstores or convenience marts in downtown.

Media
The daily *Commercial Appeal* (www.

commercialappeal.com) is Memphis's major newspaper, available all over the city. The *Memphis Flyer* (www.memphisflyer.com) is a free alternative weekly, published on Wednesday with the best entertainment listings.

Memphis magazine (www.memphismagazine.com) is published monthly and includes historical anecdotes, restaurant reviews, features on high-profile residents, and lots of advertising aimed at residents and would-be residents.

There are two independent radio stations of note: **WEVL 89.9 FM** is a community radio station that plays blues, country, and other Memphis music. **WDIA 1070 AM,** the historical Memphis station that made the blues famous, still rocks today. Another station of note is **WRBO 103.5 FM,** which plays soul and R&B.

SERVICES
Fax and Internet
Send a fax at **FedEx Office** (50 N. Front St., 901/521-0261), located across from the Peabody's valet entrance.

Most of the major hotels and attractions have wireless Internet access.

Postal Service
There is a postal retail center, which sells stamps and offers limited postal services, at 100 Peabody Place (800/275-8777, Mon.–Fri. 8:30 A.M.–5 P.M.).

Emergency Services
Dial 911 in an emergency for fire, ambulance, or police. The downtown police department is the **South Main Station** (545 S. Main St., 901/636-4099). Police patrol downtown by car, on bike, and on foot.

Several agencies operate hotlines for those needing help. They include: Alcoholics Anonymous (901/726-6750), the Better Business Bureau (901/759-1300), Emergency Mental Health Services (855/274-7471), Deaf Interpreting (901/577-3783), Rape Crisis/

Sexual Assault Hotline (901/272-2020), and Poison Emergencies (901/528-6048).

Hospitals
Memphis is chockablock with hospitals. Midtown Memphis is also referred to as Medical Center for the number of hospitals and medical facilities there. Here you will find the **Regional Medical Center at Memphis** (877 Jefferson Ave., 901/545-7100), a 620-bed teaching hospital affiliated with the University of Tennessee; and the **Methodist University Hospital** (1211 Union Ave., 901/516-7000), the 669-bed flagship hospital for Methodist Healthcare.

In East Memphis, **Baptist Memorial Hospital** (6019 Walnut Grove Rd., 901/226-5000) is the cornerstone of the huge Baptist Memorial Health Care System, with 771 beds.

Laundry
Try any of these three laundries, which are located near downtown: **Metro Plaza Laundry** (805 S. Danny Thomas Blvd., 901/948-1673), **Crump Laundry Mat and Dry Cleaning** (756 E. Ed Crump Blvd., 901/948-7008), or **Jackson Coin Laundry** (1216 Jackson Ave., 901/274-3536).

Libraries
Memphis has 19 public libraries. The city's main library is **Hooks Public Library** (3030 Poplar Ave., 901/415-2700, Mon.–Thurs. 10 A.M.–8 P.M., Fri.–Sat. 10 A.M.–5 P.M., Sun. 1–5 P.M.), a modern, new public library with 119 public computers, an extensive collection, community programs, meeting rooms, a lecture series, and more. The central library is located on a busy thoroughfare in midtown and would be a challenge to visit without a car.

The downtown branch library, **Cossit Library** (33 S. Front St., 901/415-2766, Mon.–Fri. 10 A.M.–5 P.M.), has a good collection of new releases, and staff there are happy to help visitors looking for information about Memphis. The current building was constructed in 1959.

Getting There and Around

GETTING THERE
By Air
Memphis International Airport (MEM; 901/922-8000, www.mscaa.com) is located 13 miles south of downtown Memphis. There are two popular routes to Memphis from the airport. Take I-240 north to arrive in midtown. To reach downtown, take I-55 north and exit on Riverside Drive. The drive takes 20–30 minutes.

The airport's main international travel insurance and business services center (901/922-8090) is located in ticket lobby B and opens daily. Here you can exchange foreign currency, buy travel insurance, conduct money transfers, send faxes and make photocopies, and buy money orders and travelers checks. A smaller kiosk near the international arrivals and departures area at gate B-36 is open daily and offers foreign currency exchange and travel insurance.

There is wireless Internet service in the airport, but it is not free.

AIRPORT SHUTTLE
TennCo Express (901/645-3726, www.tenncoexpress.com) provides an hourly shuttle service from the airport to many downtown hotels. Tickets are $20 one-way and $30 round-trip. Look for the shuttle parked in the third lane near column number 14 outside the airport terminal. Shuttles depart every half hour 7:30 A.M.–9:30 P.M. For a hotel pickup, call at least a day in advance.

By Car
Memphis is located at the intersection of two major interstate highways: I-40, which runs east–west across the United States, and I-55, which runs south from St. Louis to New Orleans.

Many people who visit Memphis drive here in their own cars. The city is 300 miles from St. Louis, 380 miles from Atlanta, 410 miles from New Orleans, 450 miles from Dallas, 480 miles from Cincinnati and Oklahoma City, and 560 miles from Chicago.

By Bus
Greyhound (800/231-2222, www.greyhound.com) runs daily buses to Memphis from around the United States. Direct service is available to Memphis from a number of surrounding cities, including Jackson and Nashville, Tennessee; Tupelo and Jackson, Mississippi; Little Rock and Jonesboro, Arkansas; and St. Louis. The Greyhound station (3033 Airways Blvd., 901/395-8770) is open 24 hours a day.

By Train
Amtrak (800/872-7245, www.amtrak.com) runs the City of New Orleans train daily between Chicago and New Orleans, stopping in Memphis on the way. The southbound train arrives daily at Memphis's Central Station at 6:27 A.M., leaving about half an hour later. The northbound train arrives at 10 P.M. every day. It is an 11-hour ride between Memphis and Chicago, and about 8 hours between Memphis and New Orleans.

The Amtrak station (901/526-0052) is located in Central Station at 545 South Main Street in the South Main district of downtown. Ticket and baggage service is available at the station daily 5:45 A.M.–11:15 P.M.

GETTING AROUND
Driving
Driving is the most popular and easiest way to get around Memphis. Downtown parking is plentiful if you are prepared to pay; an all-day pass in one of the many downtown parking garages costs about $10. Traffic congestion peaks, predictably, at rush hours and is worst in the eastern parts of the city and along the

MEMPHIS

interstates. But traffic isn't the problem it is in Nashville; Memphis commutes are considered more reasonable.

Public Transportation

BUSES

The **Memphis Area Transit Authority** (901/274-6282, www.matatransit.com) operates dozens of buses that travel through the greater Memphis area. For information on routes, call or stop by the North End Terminal on North Main Street for help planning your trip. The bus system is not used frequently by tourists.

TROLLEYS

Public trolleys run for about two miles along Main Street in Memphis from the Pinch district in the north to Central Station in the south, and circle up on a parallel route along Riverfront Drive. Another trolley line runs about two miles east on Madison Avenue, connecting the city's medical center with downtown. The Main Street trolleys run every 10 minutes at most times, but the Madison Avenue trolleys run less often on weekends and evenings after 6 P.M.

Fares are $1 per ride. You can buy an all-day pass for $3.50, a three-day pass for $9, or a monthlong pass for $25. All passes must be purchased at the North End Terminal at the northern end of the Main Street route.

The trolley system is useful, especially if your hotel is on either the northern or southern end of downtown, or along Madison Avenue. Brochures with details on the routes

and fares are available all over town, or you can download one at www.matatransit.com. The trolleys are simple to understand and use; if you have a question, just ask your driver.

SUN STUDIO FREE SHUTTLE BUS

Sun Studio runs a free shuttle between Sun Studio, the Rock 'n' Soul Museum at Beale Street, and Graceland. The first run stops at the Graceland Heartbreak Hotel at 9:55 A.M., Graceland at 10 A.M., Sun Studio at 10:15 A.M., and the Rock 'n' Soul Museum at 10:30 A.M. Runs continue throughout the day on an hourly schedule. The last run picks up at Heartbreak Hotel at 5:55 P.M., Graceland Plaza at 6 P.M., and Sun Studio at 6:15 P.M.

The shuttle is a 12-passenger black van painted with the Sun Studio logo. The ride is free, but it's nice to tip your driver. The published schedule is a loose approximation, so it's a good idea to get to the pickup point early in case the van is running ahead. You can call 901/521-0664 for more information.

Taxis

Memphis has a number of taxi companies, and you will usually find available cabs along Beale Street and waiting at the airport. Otherwise, you will need to call for a taxi. Some of the largest companies are **Yellow Cab** (901/577-7777), **City Wide Cab** (901/722-8294), and **Arrow Transportation Company** (901/332-7769).

Expect to pay $25–35 for a trip from the airport to downtown; most fares around town are under $10. Taxis accept credit cards.

WESTERN PLAINS

From the Tennessee River to the Mississippi, Tennessee's western plains are perhaps more like the Deep South than other parts of the state. The landscape is spare; in the heart of the delta all you see for mile upon mile are cotton fields—flat with neat rows of the bushy plants. In the south, near the Mississippi state line, piney woods give rise to the state's largest timber industry. Along the Tennessee River, man-made lakes present unmatched opportunities to fish, boat, or simply relax.

Of course, life here was not always peaceful or idyllic. West Tennessee had the largest plantations and the greatest number of slaves before the Civil War. This was Confederate territory. The war touched just about every town in Tennessee's western plains, but none more than the quiet, rural community of Shiloh along the Tennessee River. On April 6 and 7, 1862, an estimated 24,000 men were killed or wounded on this bloody battlefield. Emancipation brought freedom, but not justice to thousands of African Americans who now struggled as sharecroppers and remained the victims of discrimination and worse.

Out of the hardship of life in the Tennessee delta emerged some of the state's most gifted musicians, including "Sleepy" John Estes, Tina Turner, and Carl Perkins.

The knobby knees of Reelfoot Lake and cypress swamps of other natural areas, including Big Hill Pond and the Ghost River, are a

© MARGARET LITTMAN

WESTERN PLAINS

HIGHLIGHTS

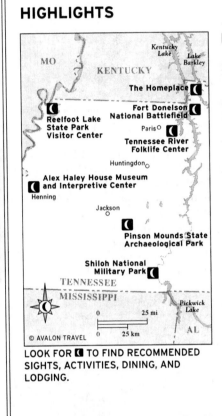

LOOK FOR **(** TO FIND RECOMMENDED SIGHTS, ACTIVITIES, DINING, AND LODGING.

(**Alex Haley House Museum and Interpretive Center:** One of the country's most celebrated writers grew up in the humble sawmill town of Henning. See the home where Alex Haley first imagined his ancestors (page 63).

(**Reelfoot Lake State Park Visitor Center:** Knob-kneed cypress trees, abundant wildlife, including bald eagles, and fresh air are elixir for those who come to this quiet corner of the delta (page 67).

(**Tennessee River Folklife Center:** Explore the forgotten past of Tennessee River pearls, steamships, and houseboats at this museum, located at Nathan Bedford Forrest State Park (page 75).

(**Fort Donelson National Battlefield:** The scene of one of the Civil War's most significant battles is also a picturesque park (page 79).

(**The Homeplace:** Located in beautiful Land Between the Lakes, this living-history museum depicts the farmer's way of life at the midpoint of the 19th century (page 83).

(**Pinson Mounds State Archaeological Park:** The sprawling and mysterious mounds at Pinson are a reminder of those who lived here before (page 92).

(**Shiloh National Military Park:** See one of the state's best Civil War landmarks (page 96).

landscape unseen in other parts of Tennessee, if not the United States. These habitats give rise to exceptional bird-watching, fishing, and hunting. Come in the spring or fall to see the area at its best (and avoid the worst of summer's heat). Late summer is the season of county fairs and other festivals, and the time when the people of West Tennessee retreat to the nearest lake, river, or stream to cool off.

PLANNING YOUR TIME

A road trip is the best way to experience the western plains; get off the interstate and give small-town restaurants and inns a try. Fresh catfish from the nearby rivers and lakes are served in traditional style—dusted with cornmeal and deep fried. Sample the varieties of hush puppies between Reelfoot Lake and Shiloh. Campers will find numerous options for shelter in state parks.

The western plains can be toured in about a week, although outdoors enthusiasts often want to budget more time to hike or fish. If you are interested in the cultural and musical attractions of the region, choose Jackson or Brownsville as your home base. If you are

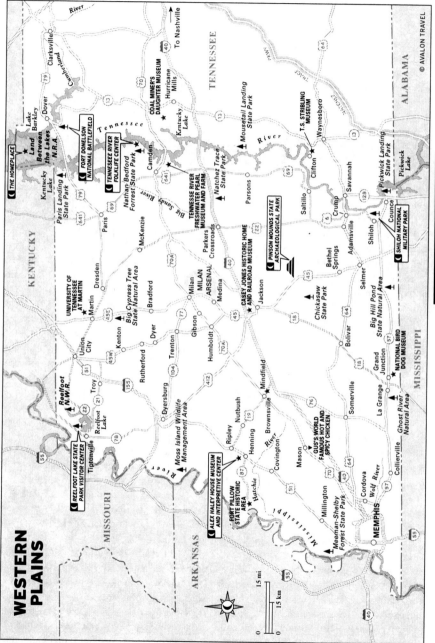

WESTERN PLAINS

interested in Shiloh and the natural attractions along the southern Tennessee River, Savannah is a good choice. For a tour along the Mississippi River, the best accommodations are found around the picturesque Reelfoot Lake in the northwest corner of the state. Paris Landing State Park is a good home base for exploring the Kentucky Lakes region.

Driving is the best—honestly, the only—way to get around the western plains. Even in the largest city, Jackson, attractions, restaurants, and accommodations are spread out. A good road map or updated GPS is all you need to find your way around, and residents are friendly and helpful if you get lost.

The Delta

Flat, spare, and rural, the delta region of West Tennessee was, and still is, the state's largest producer of cotton. Cotton fields in cultivation spread out between small towns and farmhouses. Drive through these areas in the fall, and you'll see fields of silvery white blowing in the wind. County seats of the delta have stately courthouses, enclosed by classic courthouse squares. While the region is home to the cities of Jackson and Brownsville, the delta remains rural, and the way of life is laid-back and traditional.

The delta countryside is fertile soil not only for farming, but for music, too. Blues musicians "Sleepy" John Estes, Hammie Nixon, and Yank Rachell are from Brownsville.

BROWNSVILLE

The county seat of the largest cotton-producing county in Tennessee, Brownsville was founded in 1824 and quickly became the home to many of West Tennessee's most affluent settlers. Early leaders carefully mapped out the city lots, and they were sold to doctors, lawyers, and merchants who helped the town develop quickly during its first decades.

Brownsville's first newspaper was founded in 1837, its first bank in 1869, and in its heyday it also boasted an opera house and several hotels and restaurants. It lost hundreds of its residents to the yellow fever epidemic of 1878, and hundreds more fled to avoid becoming ill. A marker

in the town's Oakwood Cemetery designates the resting place of the yellow fever victims.

West Tennessee Delta Heritage Center

Half welcome center, half museum, the West Tennessee Delta Heritage Center (121 Sunny Hill Cove, 731/779-9000, www.westtnheritage.com, Mon.–Sat. 9 A.M.–5 P.M., Sun. 1–5 P.M., free) is your best stop for understanding the special music, culture, and history of the delta region. The exhibits in its three museums—the West Tennessee Cotton Museum, the West Tennessee Music Museum, and the Hatchie River Museum—examine the musical heritage of the region, the ecology of the nearby Hatchie River, and cotton, the region's most important crop.

The cotton exhibit illustrates the process from cultivation to baling. A huge basket of picked cotton is there for you to touch, as well as the cotton both before and after being ginned. After driving past miles of cotton fields, visitors will welcome the illustration and explanations.

The heritage center also has displays about each of the counties in the region, with visitor information on each. There is also a gift shop stocked with some local-made goods. If you need to check your messages, this is a good place to take advantage of free wireless Internet access.

Right next to the heritage center's museums

is the **"Sleepy" John Estes Home,** a faded clapboard home that was relocated here so tourists could see where the blues legend was living when he died in 1977.

Estes was born in Ripley, Tennessee, in 1904 but lived most of his life in Brownsville. A blues guitarist and vocalist, Estes had a distinctive "crying" vocal style and sounded like an old man, even on his early recordings. Estes made his recording debut in Memphis in 1929, and he recorded regularly until the United States joined World War II in 1941. Estes spent the end of his life blind and living in poverty.

The Heritage Center is located at exit 56 off I-40.

Historic Brownsville

It is pleasant to drive or walk around historic Brownsville, a leafy area of antebellum homes and buildings. Each home is marked with a brown-and-white sign in the yard that is visible from the road and gives the approximate date of construction. For a more detailed guide, visit the Brownsville-Haywood Chamber of Commerce for a copy of their historical guidebook of Haywood County, which includes a walking tour of Brownsville.

Two of the city's most noteworthy old homes are the **Tripp Home** at 420 Main Street, a two-story Greek Revival home built in 1824, and the **Christ Episcopal Church** at the corner of West College and North Washington, organized in 1832. Brownsville is also home to the oldest Jewish temple in continuous service in Tennessee, the **Temple of Adas Israel** at 18 North Court Street, built in 1882.

Historic Brownsville surrounds the College Hill Center, where you will find the **Haywood County Museum** (127 N. Grade Ave., 731/772-4883, Sun. 2–4 P.M., free), housed in the old Brownsville Baptist Female College. This museum is home to a remarkable collection of Abraham Lincoln artifacts and papers, donated by Brownsville native Morton Felsenthal. The museum is open limited hours, so plan

accordingly or call ahead to inquire whether someone can open it for you.

The attractive redbrick College Hill Center, which houses the museum, was built in 1851 as the Brownsville Baptist Female College. After 1900 it became the Ogilvie Training School for boys, and later it was the Haywood County High School from 1911 to 1970.

Mindfield

Tucked next to a payday-loan storefront and quickmart near downtown Brownsville is the unexpected *Mindfield,* a collection of steel sculptures created by local artist Billy Tripp. At first glance it looks like an electrical transformer station, but this acre of creations is a remarkable work of outsider art. Begun in 1989, the sculptures will continue to grow and change until Tripp's death, at which point the site will be his place of internment. Tripp works on the piece more in the summer than the rest of the year.

Today it stands seven stories tall in places and includes messages of optimism and open-mindedness from the artist. There's an opportunity to leave comments about your impressions of the works, which are largely made from reclaimed steel and other materials. Find the *Mindfield* off U.S. 70, one block away from the town square.

Hatchie River National Wildlife Area

Just south of Brownsville is the Hatchie River National Wildlife Area (731/772-0501), a 12,000-acre preserve along the Hatchie River. Established to protect the more than 200 species of birds that winter or migrate on the Hatchie, the wildlife area presents excellent opportunities for bird-watching. You can also fish in many areas. Camping is not allowed. For more information, contact the Refuge Office located at the intersection of Highway 76 and I-40.

Festivals and Events

Brownsville hosts the **Brownsville Blues Fall Festival** (http://brownsvilleblues.homestead.

WESTERN PLAINS

com) in late September or early October, which celebrates blues and the culture of the delta. Come to hear some of the best Delta blues outside Memphis, and enjoy barbecue, regional crafts, and sports activities. The blues festival is followed the third Saturday in October by the **Hatchie Fall Festival** (www.hatchiefallfest.com) on the courthouse square in Brownsville, which offers more live music and family-oriented fun.

Accommodations

Brownsville has the greatest concentration of hotels in this part of Tennessee. Most of these are located along I-40, a five-minute drive from downtown Brownsville, some even within walking distance of the West Tennessee Delta Heritage Center and fast-food restaurants. Chain hotels located here include **Econo Lodge** (2600 Anderson Ave., 731/772-4082, $50–60) and **Days Inn** (2530 Anderson Ave., 731/772-3297, $50–60). An independent option is the spartan **Sunrise Inn** (328 Main St., 731/772-1483, $45).

In the historic downtown, try **Lilies' Bed and Breakfast** (508 W. Main St., 731/772-9078, $100). Gail Carver has two rooms in this elegant 1855 home, each with its own private bath.

Food

If you are in town on Friday or Saturday, then don't miss the weekly fish fry at **◖ City Fish Market** (223 S. Washington Ave., 731/772-9952, Fri. 10 A.M.–5:30 P.M., Sat. 10 A.M.–4:30 P.M., $5–12), on a side street in the old downtown area. Watch the catfish being cleaned and cut up, and deep fried before your eyes. Dinner plates are served with hush puppies and slaw, and you can douse your fish with vinegary hot sauce. Fried catfish, a Southern specialty, does not get much fresher or better than this.

Otherwise, Brownsville has fast-food restaurants, a few barbecue joints, a classic Italian joint, and several Mexican restaurants. **Las Palmas** (27 S. Lafayette, 731/772-8004, daily 10 A.M.–9 P.M., $8–15) is on the courthouse square and serves combination plates, fajitas, and grilled seafood.

Information and Services

The **West Tennessee Delta Heritage Center** (121 Sunny Hill Cove, 731/779-9000, Tues.–Sat. 9 A.M.–4 P.M.) near the interstate at Brownsville has comprehensive information about visiting not only Brownsville, but all the counties in West Tennessee. Make this your first stop for information about the area. There is also a better-than-average gift shop and free public Internet access.

The **Brownsville-Haywood Chamber of Commerce** (121 W. Main St., 731/772-2193, www.haywoodcountybrownsville.com) can also help with information about the region.

NUTBUSH

This rural farming community would be a mere speck on the map were it not thanks to R&B superstar Tina Turner, who was raised in and around Nutbush from her birth in 1936 until she moved to St. Louis at age 16. Turner penned the semiautobiographical tune "Nutbush City Limits" in 1973, which gave rise to a popular line dance called the Nutbush. Turner rereleased the song in 1991.

Reality is that Nutbush is too small to even have city limits; it feels much like a ghost town today. But the lone business, the Nutbush Grocery and Deli on State Highway 19 (renamed in 2001 the Tina Turner Highway), proclaims its association with the R&B megastar with a sign. But the home where Tina Turner once lived in Nutbush was torn down long ago, the lumber used to build a barn elsewhere in town.

HENNING

The tiny sawmill town of Henning is a half-hour drive through the cotton fields from Brownsville. It would be unremarkable except for the fact that it nurtured one of Tennessee's greatest writers, Alex Haley.

◀ Alex Haley House Museum and Interpretive Center

The Alex Haley House Museum and Interpretive Center (200 S. Church, 731/738-2240, www.alexhaleymuseum.com, Tues.–Sat. 10 A.M.–5 P.M., Sun. 1–5 P.M., $6) illustrates the early childhood of the Pulitzer Prize–winning author Alex Haley. This is where Haley spent his first 10 years, and he later returned here during the summers to stay with his maternal grandparents, Will and Cynthia Palmer.

Visitors tour the kitchen where Cynthia Palmer told Haley stories of her ancestors, which he later used as inspiration for his masterwork, *Roots*. The museum has artifacts of the period, as well as family pictures and heirlooms. You also hear a recording of Haley describing Sunday dinners served in the family dining room.

The museum was established with Haley's help, and he was buried here on his death in 1991.

FORT PILLOW STATE HISTORIC PARK

The drive along Highway 87 to Fort Pillow State Historic Park (3122 Park Rd., 731/738-5581) takes you through almost 20 miles of rolling cotton fields and past the West Tennessee State Penitentiary, making it unlike any other wilderness area where you might choose to camp or hike. The park, which perches atop a bluff overlooking the Mississippi River, offers group, tent, and RV camping; picnic areas; 15 miles of hiking trails; wildlife viewing; and fishing in Fort Pillow Lake. There is also a **museum** (daily 8 A.M.–4 P.M., free) that tells the controversial story of the 1864 Battle of Fort Pillow, which many historians say is more aptly referred to as the Fort Pillow Massacre for the brutality displayed by Southern troops under the command of Nathan Bedford Forrest.

There's a boat ramp on a no-wake lake, but no boat rentals, so you must bring your own. Get a state fishing license to try to catch bass, bream, and crappie.

Visitors to modern-day Fort Pillow can hike to the remains of the fort itself and see the area where the battle took place. The museum's exhibits and a short video are dated, but an interested visitor will find a great deal of information contained in them. There are reenactments of the battle in April and November. The Mississippi River Bike Trail passes through the park.

HUMBOLDT

Humboldt was chartered in 1866 at the site where the Louisville and Nashville Railroad and the North–South Mobile and Ohio Railroad crossed. It was named for German naturalist and explorer Baron Alexander von Humboldt. Farmers around Humboldt grew cotton and after the 1870s diversified into strawberries, rhubarb, tomatoes, cabbage, lettuce, sweet potatoes, and other crops. Agriculture remains an important industry, but manufacturing is increasingly important. Companies including Wilson Sporting Goods, CON-AGRA, and American Woodmark have plants in Humboldt.

Sights

The **West Tennessee Regional Art Center** (1200 Main St., 731/784-1787, www.wtrac.tn.org, Mon.–Fri. 9 A.M.–4:30 P.M., $2) is located in the city's restored city hall building. It houses the Caldwell Collection of oil paintings, sculpture, watercolors, prints, and lithographs—the only permanent fine-art museum between Nashville and Memphis. The downstairs gallery is free; the upstairs gallery charges admission. The center also showcases memorabilia from the West Tennessee Strawberry Festival, and staff can answer your questions about the area.

Humboldt's **Main Street** is home to barber shops, real estate agents, banks, and a Mexican grocery. It also has a downtown movie theater, **The Plaza** (1408 Main St., 731/784-7469, www.plazatheater.net).

Festivals and Events

Humboldt is best known for the annual **West**

REMEMBER FORT PILLOW

The earthworks at Fort Pillow along the Mississippi River were built by the Confederates in 1861, but the fort was soon abandoned so that the rebels could consolidate their troops farther south. Union forces occupied the fort for several years, owing mainly to its strategic position at a sharp bend in the Mississippi River. On April 12, 1864, there were some 600 Union troops stationed at Fort Pillow—200 of them were newly freed African Americans who had volunteered to join the Union cause.

By 1864 it was clear to many, if not most, that the South would lose the war, so when legendary Confederate general Nathan Bedford Forrest attacked Fort Pillow on April 12, it was not a battle of strategic importance but instead a fight for supplies and pride.

Accounts are that the Confederates quickly overcame the fort by land, but that an inexperienced Union commander, Maj. William Bradford, twice declined to surrender. Whether he finally surrendered or not is a matter of debate. Regardless of whether the Union formally surrendered, there was never any question which force would prevail. Forrest had more men and the advantage of surprise. With such a clear-cut victory at hand, it is no wonder that as news of the massive Union casualties emerged, the immediate cry was of massacre.

Forrest reported that a mere 14 Union men were killed in the battle, but Union records say that 300 men lost their lives, 200 of whom were black. Even Confederate soldiers writing home described the events as "butchery" and told of savagery so great that Forrest himself rode through the ranks and threatened to shoot any Confederate who stopped killing.

The U.S. Congress immediately ordered an investigation, and after reviewing a number of accounts and interviewing witnesses, declared the battle a massacre. The Confederates dismissed this as propaganda and blamed the heavy bloodletting on poor command. The precise nature of what happened at Fort Pillow remains a matter of debate.

For Union soldiers, and particularly African American soldiers, there was no ambiguity in their minds over what took place at Fort Pillow. Recognizing that official retribution may never come, black soldiers used Fort Pillow as a rallying cry in battle. "Remember Fort Pillow," they yelled on advance.

Poet Paul Laurence Dunbar immortalized the incident in his poem "The Unsung Heroes," which reads in part: "Pillow knew their blood, That poured on a nation's altar, a sacrificial flood."

Tennessee Strawberry Festival, which celebrates one of this region's sweetest crops. Established in 1934 to encourage the growing, packing, and consumption of strawberries, the festival takes place in early May at the height of the strawberry harvest. It includes a parade, car show, foot races, beauty pageants, cooking contests, and good old-fashioned fireworks. For details and specific dates, contact the Humboldt Chamber of Commerce (1200 Main St., 731/784-1842, www.humboldttnchamber.org).

Accommodations

The pet-friendly **Deerfield Inn** (590 Hwy. 45 Bypass, 731/824-4770, $55) is a standard roadside motel, with single and double rooms, cable TV, and in-room refrigerators.

Information

The **Humboldt Chamber of Commerce** (1200 Main St., 731/784-1842, www.humboldttnchamber.org) can help with information about the town.

DYERSBURG

This town of 20,000 people was mentioned in the Arrested Development song "Tennessee":

Outta the country and into more country
Past Dyersburg into Ripley
Where the ghost of my childhood haunts me

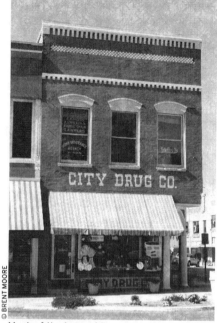

Much of the town of Dyersburg harkens back to the early 1900s.

Walk the roads my forefathers walked
Climbed the trees my forefathers hung from.

The county seat of Dyer County, Dyersburg has a handsome redbrick-and-white courthouse, built in 1912. The courthouse square is home to several antiques shops, professional services, and the **Downtown Dyersburg Development Association** (111 W. Market St., 731/285-3433, Mon.–Fri. 8 A.M.–noon), which promotes downtown and can provide visitor information.

You may not need any farming implements, vegetable plants, or fertilizer, particularly while traveling, but you may still want to check out **Pennington Seed and Supply** (214 S. Main, 731/285-1031, Mon.–Sat. 7 A.M.–5 P.M.) for its pecans and vintage look.

Accommodations

Dyersburg has a handful of chain hotels in the delta, outside of Brownsville. They include a **Best Western** (770 Hwy. 51 Bypass, 731/285-8601, $75–85) and **Days Inn** (2600 Lake Rd., 731/287-0888, $80–90).

Food

For a meal in Dyersburg, head to **Cozy Kitchen** (107A W. Market St., 731/285-1054, Mon.–Fri. 5:30 A.M.–1:30 P.M., $5–10), which serves breakfast and lunch on weekdays.

Information

The **Downtown Dyersburg Development Association** (111 W. Market St., 731/285-3433, Mon.–Fri. 8 A.M.–noon) is the best source of information about the town.

ALAMO

The county seat of Crockett County, Alamo was named for the Alamo Mission in Texas where Davy Crockett died. Its population is about 2,500.

You can see exotic animals including zebras, wildebeest, oryx, and water buffalo at the **Tennessee Safari Park at Hillcrest** (Hwy. 412, 731/696-4423, www.tennesseesafaripark. com, open daily early spring–late fall, cars admitted Mon.–Sat. 10:30 A.M.–4:30 P.M. and Sun. noon–4:30 P.M., call for appointment to visit in winter, adults $12, children $8) just outside of town. The park is the creation of the Conley family, who have been collecting and raising exotic animals on their farm since 1963. The farm has more than 250 animals, and visitors can drive a two-mile loop through the farm safari-style. Free-roaming animals come up to your car window to visit. At the barn there is a petting zoo where you can feed and touch more animals. While the Conleys have been raising exotic animals for decades, the park has been open to the public since 2007. The park is 16 miles up Highway 412 from I-40 at exit 78.

Old West Tennessee has been lovingly re-created at **Green Frog Village** (Hwy. 412, 731/663-3319, www.greenfrogtn.org,

Tues.–Sat. 10 A.M.–5 P.M., free), located between Alamo and Bells, just north of I-40. The village includes an antique cotton gin, 1830s rural church, antique log cabin, one-room schoolhouse, and country store. It is also an arboretum. The mission of the village is to preserve the rural culture of the Tennessee delta, and it has been the life's work of emergency-room doctor John Freeman and his wife, Nancy. It is open from April until "it is too cold to be out in the elements."

CHICKASAW NATIONAL WILDLIFE REFUGE

More than 130,000 people visit the 25,000-acre Chickasaw National Wildlife Refuge (731/635-7621) annually. The refuge, located 10 miles north of Ripley along the Mississippi River, is home to dozens of species of birds, including bald eagles. The refuge is a popular area for hunting and fishing—the fall squirrel hunt is one of the largest. You can also bike or hike along the reserve's 20 miles of paved and gravel roads, looking at acres of hardwood trees. The refuge was established in 1985 and occupies land once owned by a private timber company.

Find the refuge by driving nine miles north of Ripley on Highway 51. Turn left on Hobe Webb Road for 1.25 miles, and then right onto Sand Bluff Road for half a mile.

BIG CYPRESS TREE STATE NATURAL AREA

You won't find *the* namesake tree at Big Cypress Tree State Natural Area (295 Big Cypress Rd., Greenfield, 731/235-2700, summer 8 A.M.–sunset, winter 8 A.M.–4:30 P.M.); the 1,350-year-old tree, which measured 13 feet in diameter, was struck by lightning and died in 1976. But there are bald cypress and other flora and fauna here. A short hiking trail has signage that identifies many of the trees.

The 330-acre park, which is near Greenfield, is for day-use only and has a picnic area, covered pavilion, and a short nature trail. There's a lovely arts and crafts festival each October.

RIPLEY

Ripley's famous tomatoes take center stage at the annual **Lauderdale County Tomato Festival,** which takes place the weekend after July 4 every year. In addition to tomato tasting, cooking contests, and exhibitions, there is live music, a carnival, and a beauty contest. The event is organized by the Lauderdale County Chamber of Commerce (731/635-9541, www.lauderdalecountytn.org).

HALLS

American Pickers fans will be delighted with interesting antiques at a number of stores tucked away in small towns in this part of Tennessee. Perhaps the most interesting is **Murray Hudson's Antiquarian Books and Maps** (109 S. Church St., 731/836-5418, www.murrayhudson.com, Mon.–Sat. 9 A.M.–5 P.M.). Hudson has been collecting for more than 25 years and has a remarkable collection of old globes, some of them dating back to the early 1700s. He also sells old maps, books, and historic prints.

MASON

Along Highway 70 near Mason, one landmark restaurant attracts not only Memphians and residents of the delta, but also visitors statewide. ◖ **Gus's World Famous Hot and Spicy Chicken** (520 Hwy. 70, 901/294-2028, Mon.–Sat. 11 A.M.–9 P.M., $8–12) has been heralded by the likes of *GQ* magazine and celebrity chef Emeril as *the* place for good fried chicken. Gus's is set in an old frame house, modified over the years to accommodate the thousands of loyal patrons who can't get enough of Gus's hot and spicy fried chicken. Coated in batter and a special seasoning paste, Gus's chicken is fried so that the crust is crispy, the meat juicy, and the taste just spicy enough to be perfect with a cold beer. Just when you think it can't get any better, someone drops a quarter in the old jukebox and the blues fill the air. Wise diners get two orders: one to eat now and one to eat on the way home. Don't miss the quirky signage and ambience.

Reelfoot Lake

Tennessee's "earthquake lake" is a hauntingly beautiful landscape of knob-kneed cypress trees, gently rippling water, and open spaces. It is a flooded forest, eerie looking and peaceful. With some 13,000 acres of water, the lake is also a sportsman's dream: 54 species of fish live in Reelfoot, including bream, crappie, catfish, and bass. From January to March—the best fishing season—the lake sees a steady stream of visitors who come to troll its waters. The cypress tint the water a clear but dark color, contributing to the magical feel of the place.

Reelfoot Lake is home to thousands of wintering and migratory birds. Visitors cannot help but notice the daily symphony of bird calls, not to mention the sight of ducks, herons, wild turkeys, eagles, and geese around the lake. Birdwatchers have identified some 238 species of birds in Reelfoot Lake, and the April turkey hunt in the area is excellent.

Bald eagles are the most iconic of the bird species that winter at the lake, and spotting these majestic creatures is a popular pursuit January–March. Normally, the winter eagle population on the lake numbers 100–200 birds. Bald eagles had virtually disappeared from the area in the 1960s due to the effects of DDT contamination of their nesting grounds, but thanks to a nesting project started in 1988, they have returned.

Orientation

Reelfoot Lake sits in the extreme northwestern corner of Tennessee, which makes it a little bit hard to get to. Its northernmost finger nearly touches the Kentucky state line, and the Mississippi River is only a mile to the west. Two-lane state highways circle the lake; the entire loop is about 35 miles. The southern portion of Reelfoot is a state park, and the northern half of the lake is a U.S. national wildlife refuge. Several thousand residents live in lakefront communities that dot the area.

The closest town to the lake, Tiptonville, is a cluster of homes and businesses at the southwestern corner of Reelfoot. The boyhood home of Carl Perkins is found here; look for a sign on Highway 78 south of town to find it.

Most accommodations, restaurants, and provisioning locales are found along the southern shore, just a few minutes' drive from Tiptonville. The state park's Air Park Inn, along with one or two private camps and inns, are set on the lake's western shore, about 10 miles from Tiptonville. The trails and visitors center maintained by the U.S. Fish and Wildlife Service are located on the more isolated northern shore of the waters.

SIGHTS
◖ Reelfoot Lake State Park Visitor Center

The State Park Visitor Center (3120 State Rd. 213, 731/253-7756 or 731/253-8003, Mon.–Fri. 8 A.M.–4:30 P.M., free) provides the best introduction to the lake, with exhibits on its history, wildlife, legends, and ecology. You can see a traditional Reelfoot Lake boat and read the story of the local vigilantes who took matters into their own hands when the lake was threatened with development. This is also the place to sign up for popular lake cruises, guided canoe trips, and sightseeing tours.

Outside the museum are a couple of mesh cages where you can see bald eagles, owls, and red-tailed hawks. A half-mile boardwalk trail

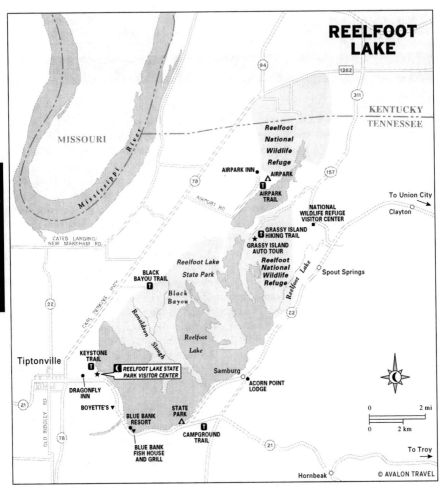

REELFOOT LAKE

MISSOURI

Mississippi River

REELFOOT
Reelfoot
National
Wildlife
Refuge

KENTUCKY
TENNESSEE

AIRPARK INN ● AIRPARK
AIRPARK TRAIL

To Union City
Clayton

NATIONAL WILDLIFE REFUGE VISITOR CENTER

GRASSY ISLAND HIKING TRAIL
GRASSY ISLAND AUTO TOUR

Reelfoot National Wildlife Refuge

Reelfoot Lake

CATES LANDING NEW MARKHAM RD.

BLACK BAYOU TRAIL

Reelfoot Lake State Park

Black Bayou

Spout Springs

Ronaldson Slough

Reelfoot Lake

Tiptonville

KEYSTONE TRAIL

REELFOOT LAKE STATE PARK VISITOR CENTER

Samburg

ACORN POINT LODGE

DRAGONFLY INN
BOYETTE'S ▼

BLUE BANK RESORT

STATE PARK

CAMPGROUND TRAIL

BLUE BANK FISH HOUSE AND GRILL

Hornbeak

To Troy

0   2 mi
0   2 km

© AVALON TRAVEL

extends out over the lake at the rear of the visitors center and is a must for anyone who wants to experience the special beauty of the lake.

Reelfoot Lake National Wildlife Refuge

On the northern side of Reelfoot, near the intersections of State Highways 22 and 157, is the **National Wildlife Refuge Visitor Center** (4343 Hwy. 157, 731/538-2481, daily 8 A.M.–4 P.M., free). Here you can see exhibits about the lake,

with a special focus on the flora and fauna of the area. Take note that the Reelfoot National Wildlife Refuge, which is, essentially, the northern half of the lake, is only open to the public for fishing and wildlife observation March 15–November 15 every year, although the visitors center remains open year-round. Contact the visitors center for specific rules about fishing, hunting, and public access to the refuge.

The wildlife refuge maintains the **Grassy Island Auto Tour,** a three-mile self-guided auto

SEASONAL WILDLIFE

There are distinct variations in the type of wildlife you will see in and around Reelfoot Lake throughout the year.

In January and February, the wintering eagle and Canada goose populations peak, and cold water crappie fishing is good. In March, the eagles begin their northward migration, while osprey return from South America. Wild turkeys are often visible in March.

Spring comes to the lake in April and May, with wildflowers in abundance and the best season for bird-watching. This is also the best season to listen for frogs. By June, you may see deer fawns, and the floating aquatic plants are in bloom.

July and August are the hottest months at Reelfoot Lake, and therefore the season of mosquitoes and deerflies. By September, it has cooled off. Fall fishing for crappie and bass begins.

During the fall, migrating and wintering birds begin to return. Short raccoon and archery deer hunting seasons take place in October; the deer gun hunt takes place in November. December is one of the best months to view ducks, geese, and eagles.

tour, year-round. The tour leads to an observation tower overlooking the Grassy Island part of the lake and is worth the detour required to reach it.

SPORTS AND RECREATION
Boating

If you can do only one thing when you visit Reelfoot Lake, get out on the dark, lily-pad-filled water in a boat. The best cruises are provided by the state park. The **three-hour cruises** (731/253-7756, adults $9, children 5–15 $6, under 5 free) take place May–September and depart daily at 9 A.M. from the visitors center on the southern side of the lake. Your guide will point out fish, birds, and other distinctive features of the lake. It is a good idea to bring drinks (a cooler with ice is provided) and snacks.

In March and April, the park offers a deep-swamp canoe float that departs on weekends at 8 A.M. and 1 P.M. The cost is $20. From January to March, special bald eagle tours are offered daily at 10 A.M.

Fishing

Fishing is the most popular recreation activity at Reelfoot Lake. With 13,000 acres of water and an average depth of just over five feet, the lake is a natural fish hatchery. An estimated 54 species of fish live in the lake. The most common fish are bream, crappie, catfish, and bass. The fishing season generally runs March–July, although some species are plentiful into the fall.

Because Reelfoot Lake is so shallow, and because of the cypress knees that lurk below the surface, most anglers use a specially designed Reelfoot Lake boat. If it's your first time, sign up with a local guide, who can help make arrangements for a boat rental and will share local fishing knowledge. Experienced guides include Jeff Riddle (731/446-7554), Craig Vancleave (731/592-2223), and Mark Pierce (731/538-2323). For a complete and current listing of local guides, check with the visitors center or tourist council. Boat rentals usually cost $50 and up per day, and guides charge $150 and up per day.

Several hotels catering to anglers offer special packages that include room, a boat and motor, bait, ice, and fuel for as little as $120 per night.

Hiking

Campground Trail: This half-mile trail begins in the spillway area and ends at the state park campground on the southern tip of the lake. The trailhead is located on Highway 21/22.

Keystone Trail: This 1.5-mile path skirts the edge of the lake along part of its southern shore. Hikers should wear shoes or boots that can withstand the sometimes-muddy path. Birds are common. The trailhead is located off Highway 21/22 and is adjacent to a large picnic area.

WESTERN PLAINS

© SUSANNA HENIGAN POTTER

the Reelfoot Lake State Park Visitor Center
boardwalk

Black Bayou Trail: This two-mile walk through the cypress swamp follows the Black Bayou Slough. The trailhead is located along Highway 78 on the western shore of the lake.

The Airpark Trail: This 1.5-mile trail winds through cypress and hardwood forest as well as open fields. The trailhead is next to the old Airpark Inn site off Highway 78.

Grassy Island Hiking Trail: Part of the national wildlife refuge at Grassy Island, this half-mile path cuts through lowland forest and over swampy wetlands. A portion follows the paved auto-tour road through Grassy Island.

Biking

The terrain around Reelfoot Lake is flat, and traffic is relatively light. Biking is a good way to get around and explore what the lake has to offer. Bring your own bike, however, since no rentals are available.

ACCOMMODATIONS

The **Blue Bank Resort** (3330 State Hwy. 21 E., 731/253-8976, www.bluebankresort.com, $70–100) has a traditional motel as well as cabins that stand over the lake, with expansive decks and a 12-person hot tub. The cabins can sleep 3–16. All rooms have a lot of exposed wood, giving the resort the feeling of a hunting lodge. The Blue Bank offers fishing packages that cost $200–300 per person for up to four nights and include gear—boat, motor, bait, and ice—for fishing. If you're just interested in a room without the add-ons, call at the last minute to find out if they have a vacancy.

The **Acorn Point Lodge** (Hwy. 22 and 1685 Lake Dr., Samburg, 731/538-9800, www.acornpointlodge.com, $59–89) has 12 rooms, half of which have lake views. Rates vary according to season and include breakfast. There are packages for hunters and groups.

For the most intimate accommodations at Reelfoot Lake, try **Dragonfly Inn** (365 Sunkist Beach Rd., 731/442-0750, www.dragonflyinnreelfootlake.com, $60), formerly Miss Pauline's Bed and Breakfast. Set in an old farmhouse, this friendly bed-and-breakfast is just one mile from Reelfoot Lake but feels removed from the crowds that exist during peak season. The four rooms are homey, and each has a private bath, individual heating and air-conditioning, and a queen-size bed. Host Marianne serves a full breakfast and accommodates anglers with early breakfasts, freezer space, and lots of boat parking in the driveway. Rates are higher during the October arts and crafts festival.

Camping

Reelfoot Lake State Park (2595 State Route 21E, Tiptonville, 731/253-9652) runs two campgrounds for RVs and tents. A small campground is located next to the old Airpark Inn

THE NEW MADRID QUAKE

A series of powerful earthquakes struck the central United States between December 1811 and February 1812. At the time there was no way of measuring magnitude, but modern scientists now say that at least three of these temblors exceeded magnitude 8.0.

The first major quake struck on December 16, 1811, and caused the ground to split open around New Madrid, Missouri. A sulfurous gas filled the air, and witnesses saw thousands of birds flying away from the area. On this day the *New Orleans*, one of the nation's first steamboats, was voyaging down the Mississippi River. The crew was no doubt alarmed to find that as they entered the earthquake-stricken area, riverbanks were shaking and waves were rocking the boat. The steamboat weathered the effects of temblors on December 19, and on December 21 the crew woke to find that the mooring that they had cast the night before was no longer secure because the very island they had anchored to had disappeared under the water.

The final quake struck on February 7, 1812, and gave birth to what is now Reelfoot Lake. The most violent of all the quakes, it caused dishes to shake in Montreal, Canada, and rang bells in Boston. The Mississippi riverbed rose and sank; boats capsized or were sucked into fissures that appeared suddenly in the earth. The quake was so powerful that it caused the Mississippi River to flow northward for a period, and it diverted a large amount of water onto once-dry land, creating Reelfoot Lake.

site on the northwest coast of the lake. A larger campground is on the southern shore near the visitors center. Rates at both campgrounds are $20 for an RV site and $8 for a tent site. Sites are given on a first-come, first-served basis; no reservations are accepted.

FOOD

Catfish and other lake fish are the food du jour around Reelfoot Lake. **Boyette's** (Hwy. 21, 731/253-7307, daily 11 A.M.–9 P.M., $10–18) is located across the road from the Reelfoot Lake State Park Visitor Center. The catfish platter is the specialty here, and it comes with generous portions of french fries, onion rings, hush puppies, coleslaw, and green beans. If you've worked up an appetite after a day of fishing, go for the all-you-can-eat catfish dinner, a steal at $16. You can also get frog legs, steaks, and burgers.

A little bit farther east along the lakeshore road you will find **Blue Bank Fish House and Grill** (813 Lake Dr., 731/253-8976, daily 11 A.M.–9 P.M., $6–20). The Blue Bank menu is sure to have something that will please anyone. In addition to all-you-can-eat catfish, fried quail, and country ham, you can choose from pasta, shrimp, steak, loaded potatoes, and burgers. The dinner menu is $8–20, and lunchtime entrées are $6–14. They also serve breakfast. The kitchen closes 2–4 P.M. on weekdays.

For a break from the rustic, drive the 20 miles east to Troy, where you'll find **White House** (106 College St., 731/536-2000, Thurs.–Sat. 11 A.M.–2 P.M. and 5–9 P.M., $14–27), open for lunch and dinner. Set in a gracious old boardinghouse, the restaurant serves uncommonly good food in a welcoming environment. The handsome white building on the town square has a lawn and adjoining gift shop, and it is a popular venue for weddings and special events. The menu includes a half dozen different steaks, pork chops, shrimp, salmon, and chicken. At lunch, choose from sandwiches, salads, and pasta.

INFORMATION

Stop at the **State Park Visitor Center** (Hwy. 21, 731/253-7756, daily 8 A.M.–4:30 P.M.) or the **Reelfoot Lake Tourism Council** (4575 Hwy. 21 E., 731/253-6516, www.reelfoottourism.com,

WESTERN PLAINS

Mon. 8 A.M.–5 P.M., Thurs. 9 A.M.–5 P.M., Fri.–Sat. 9 A.M.–6 P.M., Sun. 1–6 P.M.) for visitor information. The Reelfoot Lake State Park Auto Tour guide, a single-sheet handout available at any of these offices, is the most useful map of the area.

Kentucky Lake

The part of the Tennessee River that runs from the striking Land Between the Lakes region near the Kentucky-Tennessee line to Decatur County is commonly referred to as Kentucky Lake. The name reflects the river's breadth and its lakelike calmness, thanks to river dams built in the 1930s and '40s.

The lake provides opportunities for recreation and is home to a one-of-a-kind pearl farm. Off the water, this region includes Fort Donelson National Battlefield, a significant and picturesque Civil War site, and Hurricane Mills, the town known as the home of country music superstar Loretta Lynn.

HURRICANE MILLS

Loretta Lynn, the mega country music star, recalls going for a Sunday drive in the countryside west of Nashville in the early 1960s. That was when she and her late husband, Oliver Lynn, also known as "Doolittle" or "Doo," first saw the 1817 plantation home where they would eventually raise their family. "I looked up on this big ole hill and said, 'I want that house right there,'" she is reported to have said.

Lynn, who moved to Tennessee in 1960 at the beginning of her music career, is one of the most influential female artists in the genre. During the height of her career in the 1970s, she published her autobiography, *Coal Miner's Daughter,* later made into a film. In 1979 she was named Artist of the Decade by the Country Music Association. With the help of hipster/music guru Jack White, her music was introduced to a new generation with 2004's "Van Lear Rose."

The mansion that Lynn bought in 1966 is now just one of a half dozen Lynn-inspired attractions in **Hurricane Mills** (931/296-7700, www.lorettalynnranch.net), a town that time would have forgotten were it not for Loretta Lynn. First buying just the mansion, Lynn now owns the whole shebang: Even the U.S. Postal Service rents the Hurricane Mills Post Office from Lynn.

The town is located seven miles north of I-40, along Highway 13. Waverly and Dickson are the closest large towns.

Sights

Visitors to Hurricane Mills can tour the antebellum mansion Lynn bought in 1966, as well as a replica of her childhood home in Butcher Holler, Kentucky, and a simulated coal mine, made to look like the one in which her father worked. Guided tours, which cost $12 for adults and $6 for children 6–12, last about an hour and depart daily at 9:30 A.M., 10:30 A.M., 11:30 A.M., 1 P.M., 2 P.M., 3 P.M., and 4 P.M.

The **Coal Miner's Daughter Museum** (931/296-1840, daily 9 A.M.–4 P.M., adults $10, children 6–12 $5) is an 18,000-square-foot exhibit hall packed with items from Lynn's personal and professional life. Opened in 2001, the museum includes her tour bus, pictures, clothing, portraits, and gifts from celebrity friends. There is also the **Loretta Doll and Fan Museum** (free), located in a beautiful red 1896 gristmill.

The museums and plantation tours are open April–October and are generally closed during the winter. Call ahead to confirm.

Practicalities

The **Loretta Lynn Ranch** (44 Hurricane Mills Rd., 931/296-7700, www.lorettalynnranch.net) has an RV park, campground, and cabin

WESTERN PLAINS

rentals. There are also canoe rentals, paddleboats, and occasional concerts by Lynn herself. For something a little different, book a night on Lynn's old tour bus. For $125–150 per night, up to four people can sleep tour-bus-style, with television, a microwave, refrigerator, and coffeemaker. The ranch is open April–October.

For food, entertainment, and shopping, head to **Cissie Lynn's Country Store and Music Barn** (8000 Hwy. 13 S., 931/296-2275, daily 6 A.M.–6 P.M.). Operated by Loretta Lynn's daughter Cissie, the restaurant and music hall serves sandwiches and country-style food ($7–15). In the evenings there are writer's nights, live music, and special events.

Closer to the mansion, **Rock-a-Billy Cafe** (Stage Coach Hill, 931/296-1840, Fri.–Sun. 9 A.M.–5 P.M.) is a casual restaurant located in the old gristmill.

MOUSETAIL LANDING STATE PARK

Located on land once occupied by an eponymous river town, Mousetail Landing State Park (Linden, 731/847-0841) is one of Tennessee's newer state parks. Dedicated in 1986, this 1,247-acre park lies on the east bank of the Tennessee River in the rural and picturesque Western Valley. The town acquired its name from the large number of rodents that once took shelter in the town's tanning factories. Tanned hides were shipped northward to markets up the river, including Paducah, Louisville, and St. Louis.

The park contains several ruins from the historic era, including the original pier, a blacksmith shop, and the old community cemetery.

Recreation

There is a three-mile day-use hiking trail through the woods, as well as an eight-mile loop with two overnight shelters along the way. The shelters are well maintained and provide lovely protection from the elements. The hike is relatively easy; you could complete the entire loop in a day and camp at the park campground.

One half-mile south of the main entrance to the park there is a boat launch and courtesy pier. Fishing is popular and permitted anywhere in the park. Bass, bream, crappie, striper, and catfish are among the most frequent catches.

Also near the boat dock is a small swimming beach. There is no lifeguard on duty. A small, cold creek near the entrance to the park is ideal for wading and exploration.

Kids enjoy the playgrounds, archery range, horseshoes, basketball, and volleyball court.

Camping

There are two campgrounds at **Mousetail Landing** (Rt. 3, Linden, 731/847-0841). Rates are $16 per site. The main campground, located in a woodland forest, has 24 sites, including 19 with electricity and water. There is a modern bathhouse and laundry facilities, plus picnic tables and grills. There is also a dump station.

Spring Creek Campground has 21 sites along the banks of the Tennessee River, located at the public boat dock.

NATCHEZ TRACE STATE PARK AND FOREST

Named for the famous old road from Natchez to Nashville, this is one of the largest state parks in Tennessee. The park (24845 Natchez Trace Rd., Wildersville, 731/968-3742, www.tn.gov/environment/parks/NatchezTrace, park office Mon.–Fri. 8 A.M.–4:30 P.M.) has four lakes, including Pin Oak Lake, which offers fishing, boating, and swimming. Historically the Natchez Trace has offered horseback riding through the **Natchez Trace Equestrian Center** (731/967-5340, Mar.–Memorial Day and Labor Day–late Nov. Fri.–Sat. 9 A.M.–5 P.M., Sun. 1–5 P.M., Memorial Day–Labor Day Tues.–Sat. 9 A.M.–5 P.M., Sun. 1–5 P.M.) for adults and children as young as three years. An hour's guided ride costs $24. The center was closed for much of 2012, so call ahead.

There are 13.5 miles of hiking trails at the park, as well as a museum about the natural history and wildlife of the area. Tennis courts, baseball fields, basketball course, and an archery and shooting range round out the facilities.

The park also has cabins, a campground, a resort inn, and group lodge.

CAMDEN

The town of Camden is the seat of Benton County, whose eastern edge is bounded by the Tennessee River.

Patsy Cline Memorial

Country music star Patsy Cline, together with Hawkshaw Hawkins, Cowboy Copas, and Randy Hughes, died in an airplane crash about three miles northwest of Camden on March 5, 1963. The Grand Ole Opry stars were heading back to Nashville after playing a benefit concert in Kansas City. The Piper Comanche airplane that they were in stopped in Dyersburg to refuel and took off shortly after 6 P.M., despite high winds and inclement weather. The plane crashed at 6:20 P.M. in a forest west of Camden, just 90 miles from Nashville. Cline was 30 years old.

The site of the plane crash remains a memorial to Patsy Cline, maintained over the years by her loyal fans. There is a memorial stone, bulletin board, and mailbox where fans can leave their personal sentiments about the star. The memorial is located 2.8 miles northwest of town along Mount Carmel Road.

Near Camden

North America's only freshwater pearl–culturing farm is located a few miles south of Camden on Birdsong Creek, an inlet of the Tennessee River. The **Tennessee River Freshwater Pearl Museum and Farm** (255 Marina Rd., 731/584-7880, www.tennesseeriverpearls.com, Mon.–Sat. 8 A.M.–5 P.M., Sun. 1–4 P.M., free) is the unlikely result of one family's passion for

© DG STRONG

Even in winter, Nathan Bedford Forrest State Park is an oasis.

which is also a favorite place for boaters and anglers, as well as group getaways. There are dozens of cabins, 50 campsites, a marina, catering facilities, and a pool.

NATHAN BEDFORD FORREST STATE PARK

Dedicated in 1929 to Nathan Bedford Forrest, the controversial Confederate Civil War hero, this 2,500-acre state park offers camping, cabins, hiking, swimming, group pavilions, and fishing. There are seven cabins, each of which can sleep up to eight people, plus a group lodge that accommodates up to 64 people. The campground can accommodate tents or RVs.

There are more than 30 miles of hiking trails, ranging from easy to rugged. Swimming is good at Eva Beach, a rough sandy beach on Kentucky Lake.

The **park office** (1825 Pilot Knob Rd., Eva, 731/584-1841, www.tn.gov/environment/parks/NBForrest) is open daily 8 A.M.–4:30 P.M.

WESTERN PLAINS

◖ Tennessee River Folklife Center

Located at Pilot Knob overlooking the Tennessee River, the Tennessee River Folklife Center (1825 Pilot Knob Rd., 731/584-2128, daily 8–11 A.M. and noon–4:30 P.M., free) lovingly depicts the traditional ways of river folk. The centerpiece of the museum is *Old Betsy*, a traditional riverboat built from old farm equipment in the 1960s by T. J. Whitfield. Exhibits include photographs of a houseboat family and displays about river mussels, the pearl industry, and traditional foods and music. The museum is comprehensive but not too large to be overwhelming.

Just steps from the doors to the folklife center is a monument to Nathan Bedford Forrest and his cavalry, which defeated a federal supply depot at Old Johnsonville, near the park, in 1984. There are impressive views of the Tennessee River from the porch outside the museum, including several manufacturing plants that emit distinctly industrial smells at certain times of the day.

pearls. John and Chessie Latrendressee founded the farm in 1979 and made their first successful harvest in 1984. Wild pearls were harvested from mussels fished from the bottom of the Tennessee River for years, but the Latrendressees were the first to successfully farm the gem.

The small museum explains the culturing process, the history of the Tennessee River pearl farm, and the history of pearls. You can also watch a *CBS Sunday Morning* segment produced about the Tennessee River Pearl Farm. There is a gift shop that sells some of the homegrown pearls; others are exported around the world. For a more detailed look, sign up for one of the farm's tour packages. The full tour ($55) includes lunch and a visit to the farm itself, where you can see the phases of pearl culturing. Tours require at least 15 people, but small groups can often add onto tours that have already been booked. Call ahead to check the schedule.

The pearl farm is located at Birdsong Resort,

THE LEGACY OF NATHAN BEDFORD FORREST

Nathan Bedford Forrest is both one of the most celebrated and reviled historical figures in Tennessee. An accomplished Confederate cavalry commander and the first grand wizard of the Ku Klux Klan, Forrest has come to symbolize the Old South.

Forrest was born in 1821 in Chapel Hill, a small town in Marshall County in Middle Tennessee. At the age of 16, Forrest's blacksmith father died, and the young man became the head of his family. He had a mere six months of formal education in his lifetime, yet he became a successful businessman, primarily as a plantation owner and slave trader.

Forrest was a staunch believer in the Southern cause, and when Tennessee seceded from the Union in 1861, he enlisted as a private in the Tennessee Mounted Rifles, together with his younger brother and 15-year-old son.

In a peculiar twist, Forrest offered freedom to his 44 slaves at the outbreak of the Civil War, if they would fight for the Confederacy. All agreed, and 43 reportedly served faithfully until the end of the war.

Forrest was daring on the battlefield, often taking great risks to avoid capture and defeat. Historian Brian S. Wills wrote: "His ferocity as a warrior was almost legendary.... Forrest understood, perhaps better than most, the basic premise of war: 'War means fighting and fighting means killing.'"

Forrest was involved in dozens of battles—small and large—during the war. In February 1862 he led his men out of Fort Donelson rather than surrender. He was wounded at Shiloh and fought at Chickamauga. In May 1863, he outmaneuvered a stronger Union force in northern Alabama by fooling Col. Abel Streight into believing that Forrest had more men than he did.

Forrest's victory at Fort Pillow in April 1864 was tarnished by the deaths of so many black Union soldiers, allegedly killed after they surrendered.

His victory at Brice's Cross Roads, in Mississippi, where Forrest defeated a much larger force of Union infantry and cavalry in June 1864, is believed by many to be his greatest success.

Forrest ended the Civil War as lieutenant general in command of cavalry in Alabama, Mississippi, and east Louisiana. His last battle at Gainsville, Alabama, in May 1865 ended in surrender.

Following the war, Forrest struggled to adapt to the changes it had brought. He supported the Ku Klux Klan in hopes of restoring the conservative white power structure that existed prior to the war and served as the Klan's first grand wizard.

His business dealings floundered. Forrest lost a fortune in the railroad industry, and he spent his remaining years running a prison farm and living in a log cabin.

In his last years, Forrest seemed to reconsider many of his views on racial equality. In 1875 he spoke to a local group of freedmen, saying, "I came to meet you as friends, and welcome you to the white people. I want you to come nearer to us. When I can serve you I will do so. We have but one flag, one country; let us stand together. We may differ in color, but not in sentiment." Forrest kissed the cheek of an African American woman who handed him a bouquet of flowers, a gesture of intimacy unknown in that era.

Forrest died in Memphis in October 1877. He was buried at Elmwood Cemetery but later reinterred at Forrest Park, built in his honor, in midtown Memphis.

In the years since the civil rights movement, many people have questioned Forrest's legacy. In 2005, there was an effort to move the statue over Forrest's grave and rename Forrest Park, and others have tried to get a bust of Forrest removed from the Tennessee House of Representatives chamber: Both efforts failed.

© VIC SMITH

The Tennessee River Folklife Center is located at Pilot Knob, one of the highest elevations in the western part of the state.

TENNESSEE NATIONAL WILDLIFE REFUGE

The Tennessee National Wildlife Refuge encompasses more than 51,000 acres along the Kentucky Lake, divided into three units. The Big Sandy Unit is just south of Paris Landing State Park; the Duck River Unit is farther south, near Eagle Creek and where I-40 crosses the river; the Busseltown unit is farther south still, near Perryville and Mousetail Landing State Park.

The refuge was established in 1945 as a safe haven for waterfowl. Today it consists of several different habitats, including open water, bottomland hardwoods, upland forests, freshwater marshes, and agricultural lands. As a refuge, the first priority is to protect animal species rather than provide a space for human recreation.

Fishing and hunting are allowed in certain parts of the refuge at certain times of the year. There is an observation deck at the entrance to

the Duck River "bottoms" area, where you can see a variety of waterfowl, especially in fall and winter. There is another observation deck at the V. L. Childs Overlook at the Big Sandy Unit off Swamp Creek Road. There is a 2.5-mile hiking trail here, too.

The **refuge headquarters** (3006 Dinkins Ln., 731/642-2091, Mon.–Fri. 7 A.M.– 3:30 P.M.) is just east of Paris off Highway 79.

JOHNSONVILLE STATE HISTORIC AREA

This 600-acre park (90 Nell Beard Rd., New Johnsonville, 931/535-2789, www.tn.gov/ environment/parks/Johnsonville) is the site of Johnsonville before the creation of the Kentucky Lake, and this is where the battle of Johnsonville took place during the Civil War. The November 4, 1864, battle is noteworthy because it was the first time that a naval force was engaged and defeated by a cavalry.

The park has picnic pavilions, playgrounds, and six miles of hiking trails.

PARIS

Paris, the largest town in the Kentucky Lake region, was founded in 1823 and named after the French capital in honor of the Marquis de Lafayette. Not long after, tourists were traveling to this Paris to drink and soak in a nearby sulfur well, which was believed to have health benefits. The well was submerged by Kentucky Lake in 1944 when TVA dammed the Tennessee River.

In keeping with its name, Paris has a model of the Eiffel Tower, donated to the city in 1992 by Christian Brothers University of Memphis. Located in Memorial Park on the outskirts of the city, the model tower is surrounded by a playground, ball field, and walking trails. Don't expect to see it towering over the town, however, as the model is only 60 feet tall.

To learn about the history of Paris and Henry County, visit the **Paris-Henry**

WESTERN PLAINS

County Heritage Center (614 N. Poplar St., 731/642-1030, www.phchc.com, Tues.–Fri. 10 A.M.–4 P.M., Sat. 10 A.M.–2 P.M.), located in the Cavitt Place, a 1916 Italian Renaissance–style two-story home. The center houses exhibits about the history of Henry County and can provide an audio walking guide to historic Paris. There is also a gift shop.

Festivals and Events

More than 12,500 pounds of catfish are served at the **World's Biggest Fish Fry** (www.worldsbiggestfishfry.com), which takes place in Paris in late April every year. The tradition evolved from the annual Mule Day, when farmers traveled to the town to trade their mules and other farm equipment ahead of the summer growing season. In 1953, the fish fry was established, and it has grown in popularity every year, once the organizers started using local fish. Today, the fish fry is a weeklong event with rodeos, races, a parade, and four days of fish dinners, available for $10 a plate at the Bobby Cox Memorial Fish Tent.

Accommodations

In Paris, there are several serviceable chain hotels, but the option that allows you to really experience the area at its best is to choose from the many cabins and lakeside resorts nearby.

On U.S. 641 one mile outside of Paris, the **Terrace Woods Lodge** (1190 N. Market St., 731/642-2642, www.terracewoodslodge.com, $40) is not as rustic as it sounds, with free wireless Internet, flat-screen televisions, and views of the woods. This is a standard motel, but the rooms are clean and the service acceptable.

Food

Knott's Landing (209 N. Poplar St., 731/642-4718, Mon.–Tues. 6 A.M.–2 P.M., Wed.–Sat. 6 A.M.–8:30 P.M., $4–11) specializes in pond-raised catfish served with hot rolls, hush puppies, coleslaw, and more. You can also get a traditional plate lunch or sandwich, steak, or burger. They also serve breakfast.

Paris distinguishes itself as one of the few small Tennessee towns with a stellar (albeit small) health-food store. **Healthy Thyme** (803 E. Wood St., 731/642-9528, Mon.–Fri. 10 A.M.–5:30 P.M., Sat. 10 A.M.–2 P.M., $3–4) serves fruit smoothies, vegetarian and chicken salads, and sandwiches.

Downtown Paris has a bona fide coffee shop, with espresso, cappuccino, latte, and other specialty coffee drinks. **Jack's Java** (118 N. Market St., 731/642-5251, Mon.–Fri. 7 A.M.–5 P.M., Sat. 9 A.M.–noon) doubles as a bookstore and florist, and has a creative touch with its drink names.

For a sit-down dinner, try **Sepanto Steak House** (1305 E. Wood St., 731/641-1791, Mon.–Sat. 11 A.M.–9 P.M., $10–24), where you can get seafood, pasta, and chicken as well as steaks.

Information and Services

Get visitor information from the **Paris-Henry County Chamber of Commerce** (2508 E. Wood St., 731/642-3431, www.paristnchamber.com) in Paris.

Also in Paris, the **W.G. Rhea Public Library** (400 W. Washington St., 731/642-1220, Mon.–Sat. 9 A.M.–5 P.M.) has 22,000 volumes as well as computers with Internet access. The library is open until 7 P.M. on Tuesday and Thursday evenings.

Near Paris

The most laid-back accommodations in the area are found at **Mammy and Pappy's B&B** (7615 Elkhorn Rd., Springville, 731/642-8129, www.mammy-pappysbb.com, $95), a 1900-era farmhouse in Springville. Located about 13 miles from Paris in rural countryside, this is a real getaway. Dannie and Katie Williams manage this family property, which has been lovingly cared for over the years. Each of the four bedrooms has hardwood floors and private baths. Breakfasts include homemade biscuits, and guests are also provided an evening snack. Additional nights' stays are $80 (rather than the initial $95).

PARIS LANDING STATE PARK

One of Tennessee's "resort parks," Paris Landing (16055 Highway 79 N., Buchanan, 731/642-4311) is an 841-acre park on the banks of Kentucky Lake. The 130-room park inn is located next to a large conference center and dining room, all with views of the lake. There is also an award-winning public golf course and swimming pool.

Day-trippers gravitate to the lake itself. Fishing is the most popular activity; catfish, crappie, bass, sauger, walleye, bluegill, and striper are some of the most common catches. The park maintains two fishing piers and one launch ramp for public use. There are also more than 200 open and covered slips for rent.

The park has a public swimming beach, hiking trails, tennis, basketball and baseball facilities, and pavilions for picnics and parties.

Accommodations

For accommodations on the lake, you cannot beat **Paris Landing State Resort Park** (16055 Hwy. 79 N., 731/641-4465), which has hotel rooms, cabins, and campground facilities on the water. The 130-room inn ($60–100) looks like a concrete goliath, but the rooms are comfortable, and all have beautiful views of the lake. The three-bedroom cabins ($155–175) can sleep up to 10 people and are set on a secluded point overlooking the lake. The campground ($14.50–17.50) has both RV and tent sites, a laundry, bathhouse, and dump station.

As its name suggests, **The Reel Inn** (2155 Hwy. 119 N., Buchanan, 731/232-8227, $99) caters to anglers. The lakeside offerings here include two-bedroom cabins with washer/dryers, daily maid service, full-size kitchen appliances, and other comforts of home.

Buchanan Resort (Hwy. 79, west of Paris Landing State Park, 731/642-2828, www.buchananresort.com, $69–210) has a place to rest your head, no matter what your preference. Choices include a motel, lodges that accommodate up to 20 people, and waterfront suites and cottages.

There is no shortage of welcoming resorts with lakeside cabins in the area. Another good option includes **Mansard Island Resort and Marina** (60 Mansard Island Dr., Springville, 731/642-5590, www.mansardisland.com, $68–98), which has town houses and cottages for lakegoers, and lots of amenities including a swimming pool. There are discounted rates for extended stays. Pets are not permitted.

◖ FORT DONELSON NATIONAL BATTLEFIELD

On Valentine's Day in 1862, Union forces attacked the Confederate Fort Donelson on the banks of the Cumberland River. Fort Donelson National Battlefield (Hwy. 79, 931/232-5706, www.nps.gov/fodo) is now a national park, making this site a good choice for both history buffs and those who are more interested in the great outdoors. A visitors center with an exhibit, gift shop, and information boards is open daily 8 A.M.–4:30 P.M. The 15-minute video does a good job describing the battle and its importance in the Civil War.

A driving tour takes visitors to Fort Donelson, which overlooks the Cumberland River and may be one of the most picturesque forts in Tennessee. The earthen fort was built by Confederate soldiers and slaves over a period of about seven months.

You are also guided to the **Dover Hotel** (Petty St., 931/232-5706, Sat.–Sun. noon–4 P.M. Memorial Day–Labor Day), which was used as the Confederate headquarters during the battle. The hotel, built between 1851 and 1853, is a handsome wood structure and has been restored to look as it did during the battle. It is located a few blocks away from downtown Dover.

The **National Cemetery,** established after the

WESTERN PLAINS

© MARGARET LITTMAN

WESTERN PLAINS

The outcome of the Civil War was determined at Fort Donelson National Battlefield.

war, was built on grounds where escaped slaves lived in a so-called contraband camp during the Civil War. The camp was established by the Union army to accommodate slaves who fled behind Union lines during the war. The freedmen and women worked for the Union army, often without pay. It was not until 1862 that the Union army allowed blacks to join as soldiers.

There are more than five miles of hiking trails at Fort Donelson National Battlefield, including the three-mile River Circle Trail and four-mile Donelson Trail. Both hikes begin at the visitors center. Picnic tables are located next to the river near the old fort.

DOVER

A small town set at the southern shore of the Cumberland River, Dover is Tennessee's major gateway to the Land Between the Lakes. It is also the place where Gen. Ulysses S. Grant earned the nickname "Unconditional Surrender" during the Civil War.

Dover has a reputation for being a speed trap, so obey posted speed limits when driving here.

Accommodations

Just west of the entrance to Land Between the Lakes, the **Dover Inn Motel** (1545 Donelson Pkwy., 931/232-5556, $60–70) has both traditional motel rooms and modern cabins with full kitchens. All rooms have telephones, cable TV, air-conditioning, and coffeemakers. They cater to hunters and anglers who are going to Land Between the Lakes but don't want to camp. There is a swimming pool on the property.

Choose from a private campground or log cabins at **Leatherwood Resort** (753 Leatherwood Bay Rd., 931/232-5137, www.leatherwoodresort.com, $35 campground, $104–210 cabins). The cabins have a minimum four-night stay. Leashed pets are permitted, and there are discounts for weekly rates.

Food

As one of the last stops before entering Land Between the Lakes, Dover is chock-full of fast-food. But folks make a special trip to stop at **Cindy's Catfish Kitchen** (2148 Donelson Pkwy., 931/232-4817, Mon.–Sat. 7 A.M.–9 P.M., $12–20) for the namesake dish, not to mention other Southern specialties including sweet and mashed potatoes and hush puppies. For something entirely different, head to the **B&M Dairy Freeze** (610 Donelson Pkwy., 931/232-5927, daily 10:30 A.M.–7 P.M., $4–8), a casual restaurant serving burgers, hot dogs, and ice cream that's located just west of downtown Dover.

Located downtown, **The Dover Grille** (310 Donelson Pkwy., 931/232-7919, daily 7 A.M.–9 P.M., $5–12) serves burgers, dinner plates, Southwestern platters, pasta, and salads.

Several miles east of the town is the **Log Cabin Cafe** (1394 Hwy. 79, 931/232-0220, Mon.–Sat. 6 A.M.–9 P.M., Sun. 6 A.M.–3 P.M., $6–12). The café serves traditional Southern

UNCONDITIONAL SURRENDER

It was the day after Valentine's Day 1862, and things were bleak for the Confederate army at Fort Donelson. The fort, located on the banks of the Cumberland River, was under attack from Federal forces, and generals feared a siege.

Southern generals Floyd and Pillow slipped away overnight, leaving General Buckner, a former friend and schoolmate of General Grant, in command. On the morning of February 16, Buckner wrote to Grant asking for the terms of surrender.

In Grant's famous reply, he said no terms other than "unconditional and immediate" surrender would be accepted. Buckner surrendered, and 13,000 Confederate men were taken prisoner. The path to the heart of the Confederacy was now open, and Grant earned a new nickname: "Unconditional Surrender" Grant.

food in a modern log cabin. It is a popular pit stop for workmen; the café's breakfast will fuel you all day long.

Information

The **Stewart County Chamber of Commerce** (117 Visitor Center Ln., 931/232-8290, www.stewartcountychamberofcommerce.com) provides visitor information.

CROSS CREEKS NATIONAL WILDLIFE REFUGE

Four miles east of Dover is the 8,862-acre Cross Creeks National Wildlife Refuge (643 Wildlife Rd., 931/232-7477, refuge Mar. 16–Nov. 14 daily daylight hours, visitors center year-round Mon.–Fri. 7 A.M.–3:30 P.M.). Established in 1962, the refuge includes 12.5 miles of bottomlands along the Cumberland River, plus nearby rocky bluffs and rolling hills. There is also marsh, brush, and farmland. The refuge is an important habitat for geese, ducks, raptors, shorebirds, wading birds, and neotropical migratory birds. In January, when the bird population is at its peak, as many as 60,000 birds may be in the refuge. Mallard ducks make up the majority. American bald eagles and golden eagles also live in the refuge, along with great blue herons, wild turkeys, muskrats, coyotes, and bobcats. Farms within the refuge grow corn, soybeans, grain sorghum, and wheat; a portion of each harvest is left in the field for wildlife to consume.

A network of paved and gravel roads along the southern shore of the Cumberland are the best places to view the refuge. Rattlesnake Trail is a one-mile hiking path through the refuge. While hunting is allowed at certain times of year, camping and campfires are prohibited.

To find Cross Creeks, drive about four miles east of Dover on Highway 49. Look for Wildlife Drive on your left.

Land Between the Lakes

This narrow finger of land that lies between the Cumberland and Tennessee Rivers is a natural wonderland. Comprising 170,000 acres of land and wrapped by 300 miles of undeveloped river shoreline, the **Land Between the Lakes National Recreation Area** (100 Van Morgan Dr., Golden Pond, 270/924-2000, www.lbl.org) has become one of the most popular natural areas in this region of the country. Split between Tennessee and Kentucky, the area provides unrivaled opportunities to camp, hike, boat, play, or just simply drive through quiet wilderness.

The area lies between what is now called Kentucky Lake (the Tennessee River) and Lake Barkley (the Cumberland River). At its narrowest point, the distance between these two bodies of water is only one mile. The drive from north to south is 43 miles. About one-third of the park is in Tennessee; the rest is in Kentucky. It is managed by the U.S. Forest Service, an agency of the U.S. Department of Agriculture.

History

Land Between the Lakes was not always a natural and recreational area. Native Americans settled here, drawn to the fertile soil, proximity to the rivers, and gentle terrain. European settlers followed, and between about 1800 and the 1960s the area, then called Between the Rivers, saw thriving small settlements. Residents farmed and traded along the rivers, which were served by steamboats.

In many respects, settlers in Between the Rivers were even more isolated than those in other parts of what was then the western frontier of the United States. They did not necessarily associate with one state or another, instead forming a distinct identity of their own. During the Civil War, it was necessary to finally determine the border between Tennessee and Kentucky, since this line also marked the border between the Union and the Confederacy.

It was during another period of upheaval in the United States that the future of the Between the Rivers region changed forever. In the midst of the Great Depression, Congress created the Tennessee Valley Authority, which improved soil conditions, eased flooding, brought electricity, and created jobs in Tennessee. One of TVA's projects was the Kentucky Dam, which was built between 1938 and 1944 and impounded the Tennessee River. In 1957, work began on Barkley Dam, which impounded the Cumberland River and put an end to floods that damaged crops and destroyed property along the river.

About 25 years later, president John F. Kennedy announced that the U.S. government would buy out residents of the land between the Cumberland and Tennessee Rivers to create a new park, which would serve as an example of environmental management and recreational use. The project was to bring much-needed economic development to the area by attracting visitors to the park.

The project was not without opponents, who objected to the government's use of eminent domain to take over lands that were privately owned. Residents lamented the loss of unique communities in the lake region. More than 2,300 people were removed to create Land Between the Lakes (LBL). In all, 96,000 of the 170,000 acres that make up LBL were purchased or taken from private hands.

Over time, however, the controversy of the creation of the park has faded, and the Land Between the Lakes has become well loved. It is the third most-visited park in Tennessee, behind only the Smoky Mountains and Cherokee National Forest.

Planning Your Time

Some of the best attractions at Land Between the Lakes charge admission. If you are planning to visit all or most of them, consider one of the packages offered by the Forest Service. The discount package allows you to visit each attraction once over a seven-day period at a 25 percent discount. Another option is the $30 LBL Fun Card, which gives you 10 admissions to any of three attractions. It does not expire. You can buy packages at either the north (Kentucky) or south (Tennessee) welcome station or the Golden Pond Visitor Center.

During certain summer weekends there are free two-hour tours of Lake Barkley's **Power Plant and Navigation Lock** (270/362-4236). You must call in advance to reserve a spot and complete a registration form.

SIGHTS

Driving south to north along the scenic main road, or trace, that runs along the middle of the park, you will find the major attractions within Land Between the Lakes.

Great Western Iron Furnace

About 11 miles inside the park is the Great Western Iron Furnace, built by Brian, Newell, and Company in 1854. If you have traveled around this part of Tennessee much, you will have come to recognize the distinctive shape of the old iron furnaces, which dot the landscape in the counties between Nashville and the Tennessee River. Like the Great Western Furnace, these plants were used to create high-quality iron from iron ore deposits in the earth.

The Great Western Furnace operated for less than two years. By 1856 panic over reported slave uprisings and the coming of the Civil War caused the plant to shut down. It would never make iron again.

◖ The Homeplace

Just beyond the furnace is The Homeplace (Mar. and Nov. Wed.–Sat. 9 A.M.–5 P.M., Sun. 10 A.M.–5 P.M., Apr.–Oct. Mon.–Sat. 9 A.M.–5 P.M., Sun. 10 A.M.–5 P.M., ages 13 and up $4, children 4 and under free), a living-history museum that depicts life in Between the Rivers in about 1850. At the middle of the 19th century, Between the Rivers was home to an iron ore industry and hundreds of farmers. These farmers raised crops and livestock for their own use, as well as to sell where they could. In 1850, about 10,000 people lived in Between the Rivers, including 2,500 slaves and 125 free blacks.

The Homeplace re-creates an 1850 farmstead. Staff dress in period clothes and perform the labors that settlers would have done: They sow seeds in the spring, harvest in the summer and fall, and prepare the fields for the next year in the winter. The farm includes a dogtrot cabin, where you can see how settlers would have lived, cooked, and slept. Out back there is a small garden, a plot of tobacco, pigs, sheep, oxen, and a barn. You may see farmers splitting shingles, working oxen, sewing quilts, making candles, or any other of the dozens of tasks that settlers performed on a regular basis.

The Homeplace publishes a schedule that announces when certain activities will take place, such as canning, sheering of sheep, or harvesting tobacco. Even if you come when there is no special program, you will be able to see staff taking on everyday tasks, and you can ask them about any facet of life on the frontier.

Elk and Bison Prairie

Archaeological evidence shows that elk and bison once grazed in Tennessee and Kentucky, including the area between the rivers. Settlers quickly destroyed these herds, however. Both bison and elk were easy to hunt, and they were desirable for their meat and skins. By 1800, bison had been killed off, and about 50 years later elk were gone, too.

When Land Between the Lakes was created, elk and bison were reintroduced to the area. The South Bison Range across the road from the Homeplace is one of the places where bison now live. The bison herd that roams on about 160 acres here can sometimes be seen from the main road, or from side roads bordering the range.

You can see both bison and elk at the Elk and Bison Prairie, a 700-acre restoration project located near the midpoint of the Land Between the Lakes. In 1996, 39 bison were relocated from the south prairie here, and 29 elk were transported from Canada. Since then, the population of both animals has grown.

Visitors may drive through the range along a one-mile loop. Admission is $5 per vehicle. You are advised to take your time, roll down your windows, and keep your eyes peeled for a sign of the animals. The best time to view elk and bison is in the early morning or late afternoon. At other times of day, you may just enjoy the sights and sounds of the grassland. Pay attention to the road as well as the animals, as the car in front of you may slow to take photos of one of these magnificent creatures. You may also see some bison from the trace en route.

© MARGARET LITTMAN

See Tennessee as it was in the 19th century at The Homeplace.

Golden Pond Visitor Center and Planetarium

For the best overview of the history, nature, and significance of the Land Between the Lakes, stop at the Golden Pond Visitor Center and Planetarium (Natchez Trace and US Hwy. 68/80, 270/924-2000, daily 9 A.M.–5 P.M., visitors center free, planetarium shows ages 13 and up $4, children 5–12 $2, children 4 and under free). The visitors center is home to a small museum about the park, where you can also watch a video about the elk that have been restored on the Elk and Bison Prairie. There is also a gift shop, restrooms, and picnic area.

The planetarium screens at least four programs daily about astronomy and nature, with more during the holidays. On Saturday and Sunday at 1 P.M. you can get a sneak peak at the night sky above.

Golden Pond was the name of Land Between the Lakes's largest town before the park was created. Golden Pond, also called Fungo, was a vibrant town that, at its peak, had a hotel, bank, restaurants, and other retail outlets. During Prohibition, farmers made moonshine in the woods and sold it in Golden Pond. Golden Pond whiskey was sought after in back alley saloons as far away as Chicago. When Land Between the Lakes was created in 1963, Golden Pond had a population of about 200 people. Families moved their homes and relocated to communities outside the park. In 1970, when the historic society unveiled a marker at the site of Golden Pond, the strains of "Taps" rang out over the hills.

You can visit the site of Golden Pond by driving a few miles east of the visitors center on Highway 80. There is a picnic area.

Woodlands Nature Station

The final major attraction in Land Between the Lakes is the Woodlands Nature Station (north of the visitors center on the Trace, 270/924-2020, Apr.–Oct. Mon.–Sat. 9 A.M.–5 P.M. and Sun. 10 A.M.–5 P.M., Mar. and Nov. Wed.–Sat.

9 A.M.–5 P.M. and Sun. 10 A.M.–5 P.M., closed Dec.–Feb., ages 13 and up $4, children 5–12 $2, children 4 and under free). Geared to children, the nature station introduces visitors to animals including bald eagles, coyotes, opossum, and deer. There are also opportunities for staff-led hiking trips. Special events and activities take place nearly every weekend, and during the week in summertime.

Center Furnace

You can see the ruins of what was once the largest iron furnace in the Land Between the Lakes along the Center Furnace Trail. Along the short (0.3 mile) walk you will see signs that describe the process of making iron and explain why it was practiced Between the Rivers.

Center Furnace was built between 1844 and 1846. It continued to operate until 1912, much longer than any other furnace in the area.

RECREATION

Promoting outdoor recreation is one of the objectives of Land Between the Lakes. Visitors can enjoy hiking, biking, paddling, or horseback riding; hunting and fishing; and camping. There is even an area specially designated for all-terrain vehicles.

Trails

There are 200 miles of hiking trails in Land Between the Lakes. Some of these are also open for mountain biking and horseback riding.

The **Fort Henry Trails** are a network of 29.3 miles of trails near the southern entrance to the park, some of which follow the shoreline of the Kentucky Lake. The intricate network of trails allows hikers to choose from a three-mile loop to something much longer.

Access the trails from the south welcome station, or from the Fort Henry Trails parking area, at the end of Fort Henry Road. These trails crisscross the grounds once occupied by the Confederate Fort Henry. They are for hikers only.

The **North-South Trail** treks the entire length of the Land Between the Lakes. From start to finish, it is 58.6 miles. Three backcountry camping shelters are available along the way for backpackers. The trail crosses the main road in several locations. Portions of the trail are open to horseback riders. The portion from the Golden Pond Visitor Center to the northern end is also open to mountain bikers.

The 2.2-mile **Honker Lake Loop Trail** begins at the Woodlands Nature Station. This trail is open to hikers only. Sightings of fallow deer and giant Canada geese are common along this trail. The banks of nearby Hematite Lake are littered with bits of blue stone, remnants of slag from Center Iron Furnace.

Finally, at the northern end of the park are the **Canal Loop Trails,** a network of hike/bike trails that depart from the north welcome station. These trails meander along the shores of both Kentucky Lake and Lake Barkley. The entire loop is 14.2 miles, but connector trails enable you to fashion a shorter hike or ride if you want.

A detailed map showing all hiking, biking, and horseback trails can be picked up at any of the park visitors centers. You can rent bikes at Hillman Ferry and Piney Campgrounds.

Off-Highway Vehicles

There are more than 100 miles of trail for off-highway vehicles (OHVs). OHV permits are available for $15 for one to three days, $30 for seven days, and $60 for an annual pass; passes may be purchased at any Land Between the Lakes visitors center. Call 270/924-2000 in advance to find out if any of the trails are closed due to bad weather or poor conditions.

Fishing and Boating

Land Between the Lakes offers excellent fishing. The best season for fishing is spring, April–June, when fish move to shallow waters to spawn. Crappie, largemouth bass, and a variety of sunfish may be caught at this time.

Summer and fall offer good fishing, while winter is fair. A fishing license from the state in which you will be fishing is required; these may be purchased from businesses outside the park. Specific size requirements and open dates may be found at any of the visitors centers.

There are 19 different lake access points where you can put in a boat. Canoe rentals are available at the Energy Lake Campground, which is over the border in Kentucky. Energy Lake is a no-wake lake.

Hunting

Controlled hunting is one of the tools that the Forest Service uses to manage populations of wild animals in Land Between the Lakes. Hunting also draws thousands of visitors each year. The annual spring turkey hunt and fall deer hunts are the most popular.

Specific rules govern each hunt, and in many cases hunters must apply in advance for a permit. Hunters must also have a $20 LBL Hunter Use Permit, as well as the applicable state licenses. For details on hunting regulations, call the park at 270/924-2065.

CAMPING

There are nine campgrounds at Land Between the Lakes. All campgrounds have facilities for tent or trailer camping.

Most campgrounds are open March 1–November 1, although some are open year-round. There's a complicated formula for figuring out the price of campsites, based on which campground it is, the day or the week, and the month of the year. In general costs range $12–13 per night; RV sites range $6–32, depending on whether there is access to electricity, water, and sewer services.

Reservations are accepted for select campsites at Piney, Energy Lake, Hillman Ferry, and Wrangler Campgrounds up to six months in advance. Call the LBL headquarters in Kentucky at 270/924-2000 or visit the website at www.lbl.org to make a reservation.

Piney Campground

Located on the southern tip of Land Between the Lakes, Piney Campground is convenient to visitors arriving from the Tennessee side of the park, and, as a result, can be one of the most crowded campgrounds in LBL. Piney has more than 300 campsites; 281 have electricity; 44 have electricity, water, and sewer; and 59 are primitive tent sites.

There are also nine rustic one-bedroom camping shelters with a ceiling fan, table and chairs, electric outlets, and large porch. Sleeping accommodations are one double bed and a bunk bed. Outside there is a picnic table and fire ring. There are no bathrooms; shelter guests use the same bathhouses as other campers. Camp shelters cost $35–37 per night and sleep up to four people.

Piney's amenities include a camp store, bike rental, archery range, playground, swimming beach, boat ramp, and fishing pier.

Energy Lake Campground

Near the midpoint of Land Between the Lakes, Energy Lake Campground has tent and trailer campsites, electric sites, and group camp facilities. It tends to be less crowded than some of the other campground and has nice lake-side sites, with a swimming area, volleyball, and other kid-friendly activities.

Hillman Ferry Campground

Located near the northern end of Land Between the Lakes, Hillman Ferry has 380 tent and RV campsites. It is nestled on the shores of Kentucky Lake, between Moss Creek and Pisgah Bay.

Electric and nonelectric sites are available. There is a dumping station, bathhouses with showers and flush toilets, drinking water, a camp store, swimming area, coin-operated laundry, and bike rentals.

Boat and Horse Camping

In addition to the campgrounds already listed,

Land Between the Lakes operates five lakeside camping areas that are designed for boaters who want to spend the night. Rushing Creek/Jones Creek is the most developed of these camping areas; it has 40 tent or RV sites and a bathhouse with showers and flush toilets. Other campsites, including Birmingham Ferry/Smith Bay, Cravens Bay, Fenton, and Gatlin Point, have chemical toilets, tent camping sites, and grills.

LBL also has Wrangler's Campground, designed for horseback riders. In addition to tent and RV sites, there are camping shelters and horse stalls. Amenities include a camp store, bathhouses, coin laundry, and playground.

Backcountry Camping
Backcountry camping is allowed year-round in Land Between the Lakes. All you need is a backcountry permit and the right gear to enjoy unlimited choices of campsites along the shoreline or in the woodlands.

FOOD
There are no restaurants in Land Between the Lakes. There are vending machines with snacks and sodas at the Homeplace, Golden Pond Visitor Center, and the Woodlands Nature Station. Picnic facilities abound.

There is a McDonald's at the southern entrance to the park. Dover, five miles east, has a number of fast-food and local eateries. Twenty miles to the west, Paris has dozens of different restaurants.

INFORMATION AND SERVICES
The Forest Service maintains a useful website about Land Between the Lakes at www.lbl.org. You can also call 270/924-2000 to request maps and information sheets. The park headquarters is located at the Golden Pond Visitor Center.

When you arrive, stop at the nearest welcome or visitors center for up-to-date advisories and activity schedules. Each of the welcome centers and the visitors center are open daily 9 A.M.–5 P.M.

The **Land Between the Lakes Association** (800/455-5897, www.friendsoflbl.org) organizes volunteer opportunities and publishes a detailed tour guide to the park, which includes historical and natural anecdotes.

WESTERN PLAINS

Jackson

The largest city between Nashville and Memphis, Jackson is the center of commerce and business for rural West Tennessee. Every Pringles potato chip in the world is made in Jackson, which also hosts a number of events, including a Division One women's basketball tournament, the Miss Tennessee pageant, and the West Tennessee State Fair.

Jackson owes its existence to the railroads, and the city has preserved this history at a top-notch museum set right next to the railroad tracks. Jackson is also home to a museum dedicated to the life and death of famous railroad engineer Casey Jones, and another that zeroes in on that endearing art form, rockabilly.

SIGHTS
Jackson's city center is about five miles south of I-40, and the roadways between the interstate and downtown are cluttered with strip malls, motels, and traffic. Most of the attractions, with the exception of Casey Jones Village, are downtown on the blocks surrounding the stately courthouse square.

Casey Jones Historic Home and Railroad Museum
In 1980, the home of the legendary railroad engineer was moved from the city of Jackson to Casey Jones Village, a plaza of shops and restaurants just off the interstate north of Jackson.

WESTERN PLAINS

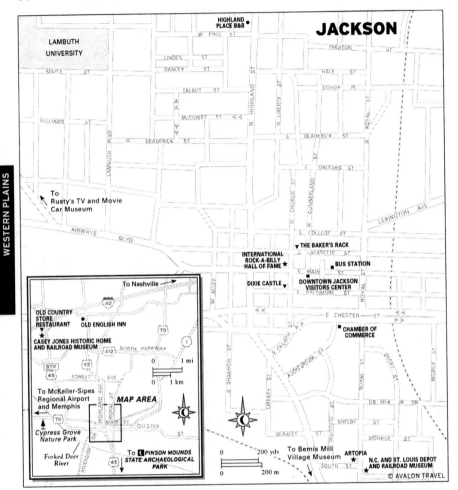

The museum includes Jones's white clapboard home and a replica of the engine that he rode to his death in 1900. The home and engine form the centerpiece of the Casey Jones Historic Home and Railroad Museum (56 Casey Jones Ln., 731/668-1222, www.caseyjones.com, Mon.–Sun. 9 A.M.–5 P.M., adults $6.50, children 6–12 $4.50, children under 6 free), which tells the story of Casey Jones's life and the legend that surrounds him to this day. Exhibits document every detail of the deadly 1900 crash that took his life, but some of the most fascinating parts of the museum deal with the legend of Casey Jones that evolved after his death. There are also elaborate model train sets that you can run for just a few quarters.

N. C. & St. Louis Depot and Railroad Museum

Jackson owes it existence to the railroads that passed through the town, and the N. C. & St. Louis Depot and Railroad Museum

© GARRY THOMPSON

The legend of Casey Jones lives on in Jackson.

(582 S. Royal St., 731/425-8223, Mon.–Sat. 10 A.M.–3 P.M., free) documents much of the city's railroad history. Located inside Jackson's oldest railroad station a few blocks south of downtown, the museum walls are covered with photographs and memorabilia of the railroads. There is a large model train in the rear of the station, and outside visitors can explore a dining car and engine.

Over the railroad tracks from the museum is a covered well whose waters once drew thousands of people to Jackson. The **Electro Chalybeate Well** (604 S. Royal St.) was discovered in the late 1800s, and its waters were reputed to cure a host of ailments. In recent years the city of Jackson built the fountain, gazebo, and benches around the well. You can drink the water from a circle of water fountains if you like.

International Rock-a-Billy Hall of Fame

As the city that lays claim to Carl Perkins,

Jackson is home to the International Rock-a-Billy Hall of Fame (105 N. Church St., 731/423-5440, www.rockabilly.org, Mon.–Thurs. 10 A.M.–5 P.M., Fri.–Sat. 10 A.M.–2 P.M., $10). This storefront museum features exhibits about a number of the genre's famous performers. There is also a room of Elvis memorabilia and a performance space for concerts and dancing. A tour with enthusiastic guide Linda McGee costs $10 and is best suited for hardcore rockabilly fans. There are line-dancing lessons Monday and Tuesday beginning at 6 P.M. and live music on Friday night starting at 7 P.M.

Bemis Mill Village Museum

The history of Bemis, a cotton mill town established in 1900, is recorded for the ages at the Bemis Mill Village Museum (2 N. Missouri St., 731/424-0739, www.bemishistory.org, by appointment only, donations encouraged). The museum is housed in the Bemis Auditorium, a large, imposing building constructed in 1922

THE LEGEND OF CASEY JONES

Casey Jones was born John Luther Jones, but he was better known as Casey after his hometown, Cayce, in Kentucky. He started as a telegrapher for the Mobile and Ohio Railroad in Kentucky and worked his way up to be brakeman, fireman, and eventually engineer. Casey had a reputation for running the trains on time, no matter what.

In the early morning hours of April 30, 1900, Jones was running a passenger train from Memphis to Canton, Mississippi, when he crashed into the tail end of a freight train that was blocking a portion of the track near Vaughn, Mississippi. Jones died when his engine, No. 382, collided with the freight train and veered off the tracks. Jones was the only person killed in the accident.

The story of Casey Jones did not end with his death, however. An African American engine wiper, Wallace Saunders, started to sing a song that he composed about the dead engineer, and soon "The Ballad of Casey Jones" was a well-known folk song. The professional songwriting team Sibert and Newton copyrighted the song in 1909, and it became one of the most famous songs in America. Neither the Jones family or Wallace Saunders ever received a penny from its success. The engineer's story also became the inspiration for an eponymous song by the Grateful Dead in 1970.

The story of Casey Jones's life and death was immortalized on television, film, and stage. His widow, Janie Jones, and accident survivor Simeon Webb remained minor celebrities for the rest of their lives.

The story of Casey Jones is told at the Casey Jones Home and Railroad Museum in Jackson.

to be the focal point of community life for the townspeople. The building is an elegant, sophisticated example of Beaux Arts design. It houses exhibits about the Bemis Brothers Bag Company, as well as life in an early-20th-century company town. Additional exhibits, with recently acquired artifacts, are in the works.

Rusty's TV and Movie Car Museum

If you care more about the car than the star, head to Rusty's TV and Movie Car Museum (323 Hollywood Dr., 731/267-5881, www.rustystvandmoviecars.com, Fri.–Sun. 9 A.M.–5 P.M., other days by appointment, $5, kids under five free). This offbeat museum just off I-40 has more than 25 cars that have been used on the big and small screens, as well as other memorabilia. In many cases, these are the real deal—cars from *The Fast and the Furious* and one of many General Lees, not just reproductions.

FESTIVALS AND EVENTS

Jackson hosts three major annual events. The Shannon Street Blues and Heritage Festival

(731/427-7573, www.jacksondowntown.com) brings blues, jazz, and other music to the West Tennessee Farmer's Market in June. The Rock-a-Billy Hall of Fame organizes an **International Rock-a-Billy Festival** (731/427-6262, www.rockabillyhall.org) every August, and the Casey Jones Village puts on an **Old Time Music Fest** (731/668-1223, www.caseyjonesvillage.com) in September.

In addition, every September sees the **West Tennessee State Fair** (731/424-0151), a week of competitions, amusements, performances, and rides at the Jackson Fairgrounds Park.

SHOPPING

Across Royal Street from the N.C. & St. Louis Depot and Railroad Museum is **Artopia** (575 S. Royal St., 731/554-2929, open daily, until 9 P.M. Thurs.–Sat.), a gallery housed in an old hotel. Each old guest room is filled with the work of different artists, and items include paintings, sculpture, fabric, and much more. There is also a salon, coffee shop, and restaurant.

The **Old Medina Winery** (2894 Old Medina Rd., 731/256-1400, www.oldmedinawineclub.

com, Mon.–Sat. 9 A.M.–6 P.M., Sun. noon–5 P.M.) has two rooms and a pleasant outdoor patio where you can taste Tennessee-made wine and other food products. Old Medina Winery is the home of Lauderdale Cellars, a winery once located in Ripley.

SPORTS AND RECREATION
Parks
A few miles southwest of downtown Jackson is **Cypress Grove Nature Park** (Hwy. 70 W., 731/425-8316), a pleasant park with boardwalks, picnic facilities, walking paths, and an observation tower.

Spectator Sports
The **Jackson Generals** (4 Fun Pl., 731/988-5299, www.jacksongeneralsbaseball.com, $6–10) play in Pringles Field just off I-40 in Jackson. A farm team for the Seattle Mariners, the Generals put on a good show for fans during their season April–October.

ACCOMMODATIONS
For the most luxurious accommodations in Jackson, if not the region, choose **Highland Place Bed & Breakfast** (519 N. Highland Ave., 731/427-1472, www.highlandplace.com, $119.50–175). Set in a stately redbrick historic home along central Highland Avenue, a five-minute drive from downtown, the inn has four rooms ranging from a three-room suite to single rooms. Each room has a private bath, cable television, and wireless Internet access. The rooms are decorated with antique and modern handmade furniture. All guests have the run of the numerous public rooms, including a living room, library, and breakfast room. It sure beats a standard hotel room. Pets are not permitted.

The **Old English Inn** (2267 N. Highland Ave., 731/668-1571, www.oldenglishinn.com, $60–75) is a mile or so south of the interstate. Its 103 rooms include suites and wheelchair-accessible rooms and wireless Internet access.

The lobby and common areas enjoy distinctive flair, including stained glass and a fireplace, and all the rooms are nicely furnished with dark wood. The Old English Inn calls itself a Christian hotel, although guests of all religious affiliations are welcome.

FOOD
Dixie Castle (215 E. Baltimore, 731/423-3359, Mon.–Fri. 10:30 A.M.–2 P.M., Mon.–Sat. 5–9 P.M., $6–14) attracts a large local crowd for lunch and dinner. This diner-style restaurant serves plate-lunch specials, burgers, and sandwiches. The food is home-style, with large portions. You'll be hard-pressed to find a table at the peak of the lunch rush. At dinner, they offer steaks, pork chops, and chicken dinners. They do a brisk takeout trade as well, and the servers are some of the friendliest in town.

Also downtown, **The Baker's Rack** (203 E. Lafayette, 731/424-6163, Mon.–Thurs. 7 A.M.–5 P.M., Fri. 7 A.M.–3 P.M., $3–10) serves a diverse menu of hot and cold sandwiches, baked potatoes, plate lunches, and a famous strawberry salads. They also make decadent desserts: Try the red velvet cake or "better than sex" cake. For breakfast, choose from biscuits, eggs on toast, oatmeal, French toast, or a generous breakfast platter with all the fixings.

In Casey Jones Village off I-40, the **Old Country Store Restaurant** (56 Casey Jones Ln., 731/668-1223, www.caseyjones.com, daily 6:30 A.M.–9 P.M., $7–12) serves specials such as country ham, smothered chicken, and fried catfish, plus burgers and barbecue. The breakfast bar is a popular choice for those with a big appetite. They also have a fruit bar and the usual breakfast choices of eggs, biscuits, pancakes, and omelets.

One of the better restaurants in town is **Candela** (575 S. Royal St., 731/554-3663, Tues.–Sat. 11 A.M.–2 P.M., Thurs.–Sat. 5–9 P.M., $7–17). Located in Artopia, Candela takes a creative approach to dining, and the results are usually excellent. Lunch features tortellini pasta, seared salmon, shrimp salad, and a variety of sandwiches. For dinner try the stuffed mushrooms, lobster ravioli, or fish of the day.

The **West Tennessee Farmer's Market** (91 New Market St., 731/425-8310) takes place under shelters in downtown Jackson Tuesday–Saturday 6 A.M.–5 P.M.

INFORMATION AND SERVICES

Maps and general information on Jackson can be found at the **Jackson Downtown Development Corporation** (314 E. Main St., 731/427-7573, www.downtownjackson.com) or the **Jackson Area Chamber of Commerce** (197 Auditorium St., 731/423-2200, www.jacksontn.com).

The **Jackson-Madison County Library** (433 E. Lafayette St., 731/425-8600, www.jmcl.tn.org) is one of the nicest public libraries in West Tennessee.

GETTING THERE AND AROUND

Jackson is located about midway between Nashville and Memphis along I-40, and most people drive here. The regional **McKellar-Sipes Airport** (MKL, www.mckellarsipes.com) has on-and-off commercial air service, subject to the ups and downs of the airline industry. Check with airport officials to find out if commercial service is available.

Photographers have been known to make a detour to photograph the iconic **Jackson Main Street Greyhound bus terminal** (407 E. Main St., 731/427-1573), with its retro art deco style. The station is convenient to several attractions and restaurants but not close to any hotels. There is daily service to Memphis and Nashville; Paducah, Kentucky; and Jackson, Mississippi.

While trains still travel on Jackson's famous tracks, there is no passenger service to or from the city.

◖ PINSON MOUNDS STATE ARCHAEOLOGICAL PARK

One of the largest complexes of mounds ever built by Woodland Indians is found 10 miles south of Jackson. Pinson Mounds (460 Ozier Rd., 731/988-5614, museum open Mon.–Sat. 8 A.M.–4:30 P.M. and Sun. 1–5 P.M., remainder of park open until dusk, free), now a state park, is a group of at least 17 mounds believed to have been built beginning around 50 B.C. The mounds were discovered in 1820 by Joel Pinson, part of a surveying team that was mapping new territory bought from the Chickasaw Indians in 1818. Early archaeological digs were carried out in the late 1800s, but it was not until 1961 that the first major investigation of the site was completed (by scientists from the University of Tennessee).

Despite continuing archaeological study on the site, many mysteries remain. Among them is the significance of the design and arrangement of the mounds and why the mound builders abandoned the site around A.D. 500. Some scientists believe that the mounds were arranged as markers for the summer and winter solstices.

Visitors to Pinson Mounds begin within a 4,500-square-foot mound replica, which houses a museum and bookstore. The museum is dedicated to telling the story of what is known about the mysterious mounds and the people who built them. The mounds themselves are spread out along six miles of hiking trails that meander through the archaeological park. Many of the trails are across open fields, and walking can be hot during the summer months. A bike is an ideal way to get around, but you need to bring your own since there is no rental facility.

Festivals and Events

Archaeofest is a family-friendly festival celebrating Native American culture. It takes place every September and includes artistic demonstrations, food and craft vendors, storytelling, flintknapping, and more. Contact the park office for more information.

Camping

Pinson Mounds has a **group camp facility** that

© JAKE WARREN

Pinson Mounds State Archaeological Park

can accommodate up to 32 people. There is also a day-use picnic area.

BETHEL SPRINGS

About 30 miles south of Jackson on Highway 45, near the community of Bethel Springs, is **Ada's Unusual Country Store** (9653 Hwy. 45, 731/934-9310, www.adascountrystore.com,

Mon.–Sat. 8 A.M.–5 P.M.), which is unusual indeed. The shelves are packed with organic and natural food items, including grains, flour, pastas, and snacks. You can buy fresh local eggs, honey, and milk; Amish cheese and cookbooks; and homemade breads and sweets. For a meal on the go, you can get cold drinks, fresh-made sandwiches, and ice cream.

South Along the Tennessee

The Tennessee River flows by Clifton and southward to the state line. It passes Tennessee's most lovely river town, Savannah, and the site of the state's bloodiest Civil War battle, Shiloh.

CLIFTON

Pulitzer Prize–winning author T. S. Stribling was born in the river town of Clifton in 1881. His works include the 1,479-page trilogy *The Forge, The Store,* and *Unfinished Cathedral,*

which portray the history of a Florence, Alabama, family from the Civil War to the 1920s. He won the Pulitzer Prize for fiction in 1933 for *The Store.* Stribling was one of the first Southern writers to speak out about issues of social conscience. He also wrote formulaic adventure novels and detective stories. His autobiography, *Laughing Stock,* was published posthumously in 1969.

A museum dedicated to Stribling and his

THE DEATH OF GENERAL JOHNSON

Gen. Albert Sidney Johnston, the Confederate commander of the western department of the army, was concentrating all available forces at Corinth, Mississippi, in early April 1862. His objective was to launch an offensive against the Union army under the command of Gen. Ulysses S. Grant at Pittsburg Landing, Tennessee, before Union reinforcements arrived.

On April 3, Johnston ordered his troops to march north, toward the engagement. Heavy rains and bad roads slowed their progress, and the Southern troops lost a day on their journey, a delay that would prove significant in the coming days.

The Confederates arrived at their camp south of Pittsburg Landing on the late afternoon of April 5, and Johnston decided to delay the attack until morning. During the evening, he and his second-in-command, P.G.T. Beauregard, disagreed about the coming fight; Beauregard argued against attack, saying that the Union army would not be surprised. But Johnston would not be deterred. He wanted to attack the Union forces before reinforcements from Nashville arrived.

As it turned out, the Union army was surprised by the Confederate attack in the early morning hours of April 6. Soldiers described the disorder and chaos of the Union camps as word was quickly spread about the advancing fighters. General Grant, who was breakfasting at the **Cherry Mansion** in Savannah, a few miles north of Shiloh, was surprised by the sound of gunfire and rushed to the scene.

General Johnston would not live to see the outcome of the battle that he orchestrated. Midafternoon on the first day of fighting, just before the Confederates reached the high-water mark of their efforts, Johnston was struck by a minié ball in the leg. His companions did not realize at first the seriousness of his injury, and neither did Johnston. But at 2:45 P.M. on April 6, the Confederate general died, passing command to Beauregard.

Johnston was the highest-ranking officer on either side of the Civil War to be killed in active duty.

life's work is located in a building that shares space with the Clifton Public Library. This 1924 Craftsman bungalow is where Stribling and his wife, Lou Ella, lived in their retirement. The museum includes Stribling's typewriter, Bible, papers, and other personal articles. The **T. S. Stribling Museum** (300 E. Water St., 931/676-3678, Tues.–Fri. 11:30 A.M.–6:30 P.M., free) is operated by the City of Clifton. The museum/library has an ongoing book sale to raise funds for its work.

SAVANNAH

A quaint town on the eastern bank of the Tennessee River, Savannah has historic homes, a good museum, and the greatest selection of restaurants and accommodations in this part of the state. You can guess what is on the menu as it is known as the Catfish Capital of the World.

In its early life, the town was Rudd's Ferry, named for James Rudd, who operated a ferry across the river. The ferry was taken over by David Robinson, whose wife is said to have renamed the town Savannah after her hometown in Georgia. In 1830, Savannah became the seat of Hardin County and soon developed a reputation as a wealthy, cultured town.

Tennessee River Museum

Savannah is a river town, and the mighty Tennessee River is one of its main attractions. The Tennessee River Museum (507 Main St., 731/925-2364, Mon.–Sat. 9 A.M.–5 P.M., Sun. 1–5 P.M., adults $3, kids free) documents the history of the region and the river. Exhibits detail the prehistoric peoples of the region and include an original red stone effigy pipe found inside one of the Shiloh Indian Mounds a few miles south. There are also exhibits on Shiloh and the river during the Civil War, riverboats, and the economic uses of the river, including pearl farming and mussels. One of the most interesting exhibits features receipts issued by Savannah merchants to the U.S. Army party that was escorting 2,500 Cherokee Indians down the river on the Trail of Tears in 1838.

The museum is an informative first stop for visitors to the area, and staff can provide information about other area attractions. Through a partnership with Shiloh National Military Park, guests who show their Shiloh parking pass receive free entry to the museum.

Historic Homes

David Robinson built the **Cherry Mansion** (265 W. Main St.) on the riverbank, on top of what historians believe was an Indian mound. Robinson gave the mansion to his daughter when she married William H. Cherry, for whom it was named. The house, which is closed to the public, is where U.S. general Ulysses S. Grant stayed during the days leading up to the Battle of Shiloh. Cherry was a noted Union sympathizer, and the mansion remained a Union headquarters and field hospital during the war. Although the house is privately owned, visitors are welcome to stop and look. There is a river overlook next door.

Savannah was settled between 1830 and 1850, but many of the old houses were damaged or destroyed during the Civil War. However, beautiful homes were rebuilt, and many of these remain in the leafy residential area just north of Savannah's Main Street. The homes are elegant examples of fine homes of the late 19th century.

Pick up a guide to the **Savannah Walking Tour** at the Tennessee River Museum (507 Main St., 731/925-2364).

Haley Memorial

Savannah is where the paternal grandparents of

Pulitzer Prize–winning author Alex Haley are buried. Alex Haley Sr. operated Rudd's Ferry, and his wife, Queen Haley, worked in the Cherry Mansion for the Cherry family. Haley's novel *Queen* was inspired by his grandmother's life. The couple's shared tombstone is located in the Savannah Cemetery. To find the Haley Memorial, take Cherry Street from downtown Savannah and over a small bridge and enter the cemetery. Take the first gravel road to your right, and then walk over the hill, taking a right at the Y. The Haleys, as well as Alex Haley Sr.'s first wife, Tennie, share a gravestone.

Accommodations

You can get a clean, comfortable bed at the **Savannah Lodge** (585 Pickwick St., 731/925-8586, www.savannahlodge.net, $35–55), a motel that boasts the basics for its guests, as well as amenities like a swimming pool. Pets are allowed. Several national chains also have locations in Savannah.

Food

Worleybird Café (990 Pickwick St., 731/926-4882, Mon.–Sat. 5 A.M.–9 P.M., Sun. 5 A.M.–2 P.M., $5–12) is a popular choice for Savannah's locals. Named for beloved son of the soil, country musician Daron Worley, the café serves sandwiches, Cajun catfish, steaks, chicken cordon bleu, and salads, plus eggs, biscuits, and pancakes in the morning.

Another good choice for home-style cooking in Savannah is **Toll House Restaurant** (610 Wayne Rd., 731/925-5128, Mon.–Sat. 5 A.M.–8 P.M., Sun. 6 A.M.–2 P.M., $4–9), whose home fries and eggs draw a crowd in the morning. At lunch and dinner, there is an ample buffet with traditional favorites like macaroni and cheese, fried catfish, and beef tips.

For a more refined dining experience, go to the **Uptown Bistro** (390 Main St., 731/926-1911, Mon.–Sat. 11 A.M.–8 P.M., $12–19), a wine bar and bistro with seafood, pasta, and steak, as well as superb desserts, such as the Oreo cake.

Information

Stop at the **Tennessee River Museum** (507 Main St., 731/925-2364, Mon.–Sat. 9 A.M.–5 P.M., Sun. 1–5 P.M.) to pick up maps and other information about Savannah.

You can also contact the **Hardin County Convention and Visitors Bureau** (731/925-8181, www.tourhardincounty.org) for information. For information on the Savannah Historic District, visit www.savannahmainstreet.org.

◖ SHILOH NATIONAL MILITARY PARK

The Shiloh National Military Park (1055 Pittsburg Landing Rd., 731/689-5696, daily 8 A.M.–5 P.M., closed Christmas Day, free) is set along the western shore of the Tennessee River about eight miles south of Crump. The Battle of Shiloh is one of the most remembered of the Civil War; it was the battle that demonstrated to both North and South that the war would be a longer and harder fight than either had imagined. Shiloh today is a landscape of alternating open fields and wooded forest, populated by hundreds of monuments to soldiers who fought and died at Shiloh on April 6–7, 1862. The peacefulness of the present brings into even greater focus the violence of the battle that took place here almost 150 years ago and claimed nearly 24,000 casualties.

You can drive around the battlefield, but some of the most important sites are a short walk from the road. At the visitors center there is a small museum where you can watch a film, *Shiloh-Fiery Trial,* about the battle.

Sights within the park include the peach orchard, now being regrown, where soldiers described the peach blossoms falling like snow on the dead and injured; the "bloody pond," where injured men crawled for water and, in some cases, to die; and the Hornet's Nest, the site of some of the most furious fighting.

The 10-acre **Shiloh National Cemetery** is located next to the visitors center. Two-thirds of the 3,695 bodies interred here are unidentified. Most are Union soldiers killed at Shiloh, but there are others from nearby battles, the Spanish-American War, both World Wars, and the Revolutionary War. The Confederate dead were buried in five trenches around the battlefield and remain there today.

Nearly 800 years before the Civil War, the riverbank near present-day Shiloh was home to a mound-building Mississippian Indian community. The **Shiloh Indian Mounds** that they left behind sit along the west bluff of the riverbank and are one of the largest mound groups in the country. A remarkable effigy pipe was discovered here in the 1890s and is on display at the Tennessee River Museum in Savannah. The mounds are accessible on foot from two points in the park.

Practicalities

A printed guide and map to the battlefield is available at the visitors center, and it takes about an hour to follow its path. For a more detailed examination, you can buy an audio tour from the park bookstore for $12. This tour takes about two hours to complete and includes narratives by soldiers, historians, and civilians.

The bookstore is one of the best in the area and has an extensive collection of books on the Civil War, Tennessee, Native Americans, and African American history.

There are snack and drink vending machines at the visitors center and a picnic area in the park. The closest restaurants are in Shiloh, Savannah, and Counce. For accommodations, look in Savannah.

With its miles of flat roads and restrained traffic, Shiloh is a good place to bicycle. There are no rental facilities nearby, however, so bring your own wheels.

SHILOH

There is not much to the modern town of Shiloh, except a few souvenir shops and one excellent catfish restaurant that has been serving visitors since 1938. **⟨ World Famous Hagy's Catfish Restaurant** (off Hwy. 22, 731/689-3327, Tues.–Sat. 11 A.M.–10 P.M., Sun. noon–9 P.M., $9–15) is set off by itself in a beautiful clearing overlooking the Tennessee River. You can stretch your legs with a walk down to the water's edge. Hagy's menu has fried and grilled catfish, plus other favorites like chicken and steak. But choose the catfish, which is nicely seasoned and expertly fried. It comes with hush puppies and coleslaw. This will be a meal to remember.

Find Hagy's by looking for the large sign for the turnoff along Highway 22 on the northern side of Shiloh National Military Park.

PICKWICK LANDING STATE PARK

Pickwick Landing was a riverboat stop from the 1840s until the 1930s, when Pickwick Dam was built and the lake formed. Pickwick Lake was created in December 1937 when the Tennessee Valley Authority dammed the Tennessee and flooded farmland in the valley. The lake was dedicated in 1940, and a crowd of 30,000 people attended the services on the southern earth dam. Today it attracts vacationers from around the region who enjoy the laid-back atmosphere and top-flight bass fishing.

The lake lies in Tennessee, Alabama, and Mississippi and is one of the premier spots for recreation in the area. Boating, fishing, and swimming are especially popular. There are several nearby golf courses and opportunities to camp, hunt, and hike.

Pickwick Landing State Park (Hwy. 57, 731/689-3129) is one of Tennessee's resort parks, with a modern hotel, conference center, golf course, and marina.

Hiking

There is an easy three-mile hiking trail that meanders along the lakeshore.

Golf

The Pickwick Landing State Park golf course is a par 72 champion's 18-hole course. The pro shop rents clubs and carts, and sells golf accessories. Call 731/689-3149 to reserve a tee time. Greens fees range $13–22, depending on the season and day of the week.

Boating

Pleasure riding, sailing, waterskiing, paddling, and fishing are all popular activities on Pickwick Lake. There are three public boat-launch ramps at Pickwick Landing State Park, and marine fuel and other boating items are available from the park marina.

You can rent a pontoon boat from **Pickwick Boat Rentals** (731/689-5359, www.pickwickboatrentalsinc.com) starting at $225.

Fishing

Fishing on Pickwick Lake is best in the spring and fall. Conditions here include shallow stump flats, well-defined channels, active feeder creeks, steeply falling bluffs, rocky ledges, and long grass beds.

Pickwick Outdoors, Inc. (877/214-4924, www.pickwickoutdoors.com) organizes fishing vacations for groups. For a fishing guide, contact **Big Orange Guide Service** (731/689-3074) or **Rick Matlock's Guide Service** (731/689-5382).

Swimming

Pickwick Landing State Park has three swimming beaches. Circle Beach and Sandy Beach are in the day-use area; Bruton Beach is in the primitive area, which is located across the lake from the main park.

Accommodations

⟨ Pickwick Landing State Resort Park (Hwy. 57, 731/689-3135, rooms $70–80, cabins $100–125, campsites under $20) is the home of one of Tennessee's newest state park inns and conference centers. The modern hotel has 119

WESTERN PLAINS

rooms, each with a balcony looking out over the lake and the dam. Cabins and campsites are also available. There is a pool and a 135-seat restaurant at the inn, which serves three meals a day, with an emphasis on Southern cuisine.

COUNCE

This humble town is the western gateway to Pickwick Lake. It is also a hub in the region's hardwood timber industry, and you will smell the distinctive scent of the local paper plant at certain times of the day.

Accommodations

If you're planning to stay more than a few days at Pickwick Lake, consider renting a cabin. **Pickwick Lake Cabin Rentals** (11268 Hwy. 57, 731/689-0400, www.pickwick-lakecabins.com) represents the owners of two dozen one-, two-, and three-bedroom cabins on and around the lake. Lakefront cabins will cost $300–400 per night, water-view cabins will cost $175–300, and cabins off the water cost $100–200. Many lakefront cabins come

with a private dock and can accommodate large groups.

Food

Don't be mistaken by the rustic appearance of the █ **Broken Spoke** (7405 Hwy. 57, 731/689-3800, www.brokenspokerestaurant.com, Wed.–Sat. 11 A.M.–10 P.M., $12–27). This is the most upscale and creative dining around Pickwick Lake. The decor is comfortably eclectic but not trashy, and there is tasteful live music several nights a week. The menu is remarkably diverse: You can choose from catfish, po'boys, and burgers, or steaks, pork chops, and chicken cooked expertly on the grill. There are also salads, pasta, and daily specials. Come with an appetite—there are no small portions. The adjacent bar is a popular hangout spot any night of the week, and **Mombie's Pizza** (731/689-8646, Tues.–Sat. 11 A.M.–10 P.M., $9–15), right next door, serves the best pizza, burgers, and wings in Pickwick. You will find the Broken Spoke and Mombie's one mile west of the dam on Highway 57.

Southwestern Tennessee

The southernmost stretch of West Tennessee spans Adamsville in the east to La Grange in the west. Here you'll find a museum dedicated to sheriff Buford Pusser, another dedicated to bird dogs, and one of the loveliest small towns in all of Tennessee.

Information

Seven Tennessee counties have come together to form the **Tourism Association of Southwest Tennessee** (866/261-7534, www.tast.tn.org), which produces brochures and stocks information stands at interstate rest stops and other crossroads. Their guide to the region has helpful listings and a map.

ADAMSVILLE

Famed McNairy County sheriff Buford Pusser worked in Selmer, the McNairy County seat, but he lived in Adamsville, a small town a few miles down Highway 45. Fans of Pusser and the movies that his legacy inspired, starting with the 1973 film *Walking Tall,* can learn more about his life at the **Sheriff Buford Pusser Home and Museum** (342 Pusser St., 731/632-4080, www.bufordpussermuseum.com, Mon.–Fri. 11 A.M.–5 P.M., Sat. 9 A.M.–5 P.M., Sun. 1–5 P.M., $5). Pusser earned a reputation as a no-nonsense lawman during his eight-year career as sheriff. He was famous for raiding moonshine stills and for fighting criminals with little regard for his own personal safety. In 1967 his wife, Pauline, was killed in an ambush when she was riding along with him in his patrol car. Seven years later, Pusser was killed in a single-car accident while he was driving home from the McNairy County Fair in Selmer. When Pusser died, hundreds of people came to his funeral. Elvis Presley visited the family privately to offer his condolences.

The home and museum features a video about Pusser's life, family memorabilia, and two cars that Pusser used.

Shiloh Golf Course and Restaurant (2915 Caney Branch Rd., 731/632-0678) in Adamsville is a par 71 course and driving range.

SELMER

In Selmer, the McNairy County seat, you can see the courthouse where Buford Pusser worked, and where Mary Winkler was put on trial in 2007 for the murder of her preacher husband, Matthew Winkler.

This quiet town is also home to the **McNairy County Historical Museum** (114 N. 3rd St., 731/646-0018, Sat. 10 A.M.–4 P.M., Sun. 1–4 P.M., free), nestled in the old Ritz theater. Exhibits are dedicated to schools, the Civil War, churches, the healing arts, business, and agriculture.

Selmer is also famous for its slugburgers, deep-fried grain burgers that are sold at lunch counters around town.

LA GRANGE

La Grange, a mere speck of civilization 50 miles east of Memphis, feels like the town that time forgot. Old homes—some elegant, some ramshackle—line narrow drives. The post office, town office, and an old-fashioned country store constitute the business district.

La Grange, named in honor of the Marquis de Lafayette's ancestral home in France, seemed destined for great things when it was chartered in 1829. Its population quickly swelled to more than 3,000. The first Episcopal church

in West Tennessee was founded here, and in 1835 stockholders chartered the La Grange & Memphis Railway. The plans for a railroad faltered, however, and La Grange suffered from Union occupation during most of the Civil War. A tornado destroyed part of the town in 1900, and La Grange lost its telegraph station and express mail delivery to nearby Grand Junction. Hopes for La Grange to grow into a city dwindled.

Despite its size, La Grange was and is known for a special refinement and pursuit of the arts and education. In 1855, the La Grange Female College and the La Grange Synodical College for Men were chartered. The town's local newspapers, *The Monitor* and, later, the *Spirit of the Age,* were respected in the region. During the Civil War, La Grange native Lucy Pickens was depicted on the face of the Confederate $1 note and three different $100 notes. Pickens, whose childhood home at 290 Pine Street is still standing, was known as the Queen of the Confederacy.

Sights

In 1998, La Grange dedicated a 2.5-ton bronze and limestone monument to the nearby Wolf River. The **Wolf River Monument,** located near the post office and fire department, was rendered in the shape of a wolf's head and was created by Memphis sculptor Roy Tamboli.

Unfortunately, since the closure in 2007 of Cogbill's Store and Museum, there is not much to do here except look. If you come by on Saturday morning, stop at the La Grange General Store, which is part of the **La Grange Inn** (240 Pine St., 901/878-1000). Both are open by appointment. The town office is open weekday mornings.

Despite the dearth of outright attractions, La Grange, also called La Belle Village, delivers an experience unlike any other town in this part of Tennessee. Its lovingly preserved antebellum homes, rural landscape, and charming people are unique and worth seeing.

WESTERN PLAINS

Ghost River State Natural Area

The Ghost River is a 14-mile section of the Wolf River that meanders through bottomland forest, cypress-tupelo swamps, and open marshes. The river got its name from the loss of river current as the water flows through marshes and swamps.

About a three-mile drive south of La Grange you can hike or canoe in the Ghost River State Natural Area. To find the 600-foot boardwalk and hiking trail, drive south from La Grange on Yager Road, and then turn west on Beasley Road. The parking area is about 1.5 miles down the road. There is another parking area and a place to put in a canoe along Yager Road, and a marked canoe path so you don't get lost in the swamp. There is another parking area at the canoe take-out on Bateman Road. Grab a map from the La Grange town office or from the State of Tennessee website (www.state.tn.us).

Information

La Grange City Hall (20 Main St., 901/878-1246, Mon.–Fri. 8 A.M.–noon) is the best source of information about the town. They can provide you with a large fold-out map of the town's historic homes.

GRAND JUNCTION

A few miles east of La Grange on Highway 57 is the **National Bird Dog Museum** (5050 Hwy. 57 W., 731/764-2058, Tues.–Fri. 10 A.M.–2 P.M., Sat. 10 A.M.–4 P.M., Sun. 1–4 P.M., free). The collection includes paintings and photographs of champion sporting dogs, plus lots of taxidermy. There's a gift shop for souvenirs for the dog lover in your life. The National Field Trials take place just down the road at the Ames Plantation.

CHICKASAW STATE PARK

Named for the Indians who once lived and hunted in this part of Tennessee, Chickasaw State Park (20 Cabin Ln., Henderson, 731/989-5141, www.tn.gov/environment/parks/Chickasaw, daily 6 A.M.–10 P.M.) encompasses Lake Placid and a golf course. The 14,400-acre park lies midway between Jackson and Bolivar. There are more than four miles of roads for hiking or biking, plus tennis courts, an archery range, horseback riding, campsites, and a 40-room inn. Rowboats and pedal boats are available for rental here, or you can bring your own kayak or paddleboard. A 100-seat restaurant serves Southern specialties.

Bear Trace at Chickasaw (9555 State Rte. 100, 731/989-4700, www.beartrace.com) is par 72 Jack Nicklaus golf course with natural beauty and challenging holes.

BIG HILL POND STATE PARK

Big Hill Pond was created in 1853 when dirt was removed from a borrow pit to build a levee across the Tuscumbia and Cypress Creek bottoms for the Memphis to Charleston Railroad. Over the years, a grove of cypress trees have grown in and around the 35-acre pond.

The centerpiece of the state park (11701 Hwy. 57, 731/645-7967) is the boardwalk through the scenic swamp and the observation tower, which provides views of the swamp and lake. There are 30 miles of hiking trails, 14 miles of horseback riding and mountain bike trails, a campground with 30 sites, a picnic area, and opportunities to fish and hunt.

There's no backcountry camping allowed here, but there are four camp shelters.

www.moon.com

DESTINATIONS | ACTIVITIES | BLOGS | MAPS | BOOKS

MOON.COM is ready to help plan your next trip! Filled with fresh trip ideas and strategies, author interviews, informative travel blogs, a detailed map library, and descriptions of all the Moon guidebooks, Moon.com is all you need to get out and explore the world—or even places in your own backyard. While at Moon.com, sign up for our monthly e-newsletter for updates on new releases, travel tips, and expert advice from our on-the-go Moon authors. As always, when you travel with Moon, expect an experience that is uncommon and truly unique.

KEEP UP WITH MOON ON FACEBOOK AND TWITTER
JOIN THE MOON PHOTO GROUP ON FLICKR

MAP SYMBOLS

Expressway		Highlight		Airfield		Golf Course
Primary Road	○	City/Town		Airport		Parking Area
Secondary Road	◉	State Capital	▲	Mountain		Archaeological Site
Unpaved Road	⊛	National Capital	+	Unique Natural Feature		Church
Trail	★	Point of Interest				Gas Station
Ferry	•	Accommodation		Waterfall		Glacier
Railroad	▼	Restaurant/Bar	▲	Park		Mangrove
Pedestrian Walkway	■	Other Location		Trailhead		Reef
Stairs	Λ	Campground		Skiing Area		Swamp

CONVERSION TABLES

°C = (°F - 32) / 1.8
°F = (°C x 1.8) + 32
1 inch = 2.54 centimeters (cm)
1 foot = 0.304 meters (m)
1 yard = 0.914 meters
1 mile = 1.6093 kilometers (km)
1 km = 0.6214 miles
1 fathom = 1.8288 m
1 chain = 20.1168 m
1 furlong = 201.168 m
1 acre = 0.4047 hectares
1 sq km = 100 hectares
1 sq mile = 2.59 square km
1 ounce = 28.35 grams
1 pound = 0.4536 kilograms
1 short ton = 0.90718 metric ton
1 short ton = 2,000 pounds
1 long ton = 1.016 metric tons
1 long ton = 2,240 pounds
1 metric ton = 1,000 kilograms
1 quart = 0.94635 liters
1 US gallon = 3.7854 liters
1 Imperial gallon = 4.5459 liters
1 nautical mile = 1.852 km

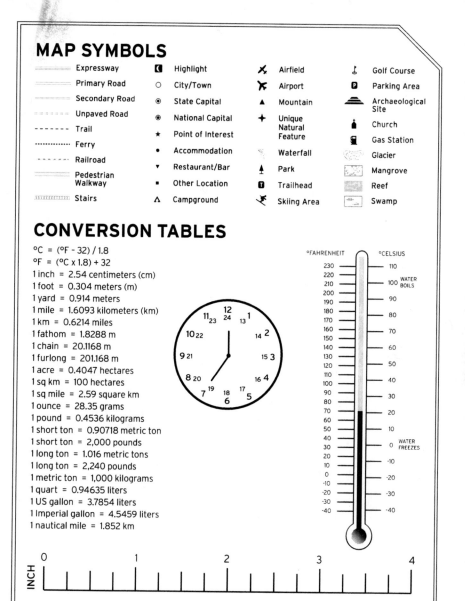

MOON SPOTLIGHT MEMPHIS
Avalon Travel
a member of the Perseus Books Group
1700 Fourth Street
Berkeley, CA 94710, USA
www.moon.com

Editor: Leah Gordon
Series Manager: Kathryn Ettinger
Copy Editor: Justine Rathbun
Graphics & Production Coordinator: Domini Dragoone
Cover Designer: Domini Dragoone
Map Editor: Albert Angulo
Cartographers: Kaitlin Jaffe, Heather Sparks

ISBN: 978-1-61238-152-7

Text © 2013 by Margaret Littman.
Maps © 2013 by Avalon Travel.
All rights reserved.

Front cover photo: night time on Beale Street in
Memphis, © Bill Bachmann/painetworks.com
Title page photo: downtown Memphis from Mud
Island River Park, © Doug Force/123RF

Printed in the United States.

All recommendations, including those for sights,
activities, hotels, restaurants, and shops, are based
on each author's individual judgment. We do not
accept payment for inclusion in our travel guides,
and our authors don't accept free goods or services
in exchange for positive coverage.

Although every effort was made to ensure that
the information was correct at the time of going to
press, the author and publisher do not assume and
hereby disclaim any liability to any party for any
loss or damage caused by errors, omissions, or any
potential travel disruption due to labor or financial
difficulty, whether such errors or omissions result
from negligence, accident, or any other cause.

KEEPING CURRENT

If you have a favorite gem you'd like to see included in the next edition, or see anything
that needs updating, clarification, or correction, please drop us a line. Send your comments via email to feedback@moon.com, or use the address above.

ABOUT THE AUTHOR

Margaret Littman

© MARK BENNINGTON

Margaret Littman is both an old-timer and a relative newcomer to Tennessee. After graduating from Vanderbilt University, she left Tennessee for points north over the course of her writing career. But after 17 years she could no longer resist the siren song of the Parthenon, bluegrass music, or fried pickles, so she returned to Nashville, where she writes about Music City, travel, food, pets, and more. An avid stand-up paddler, she loves being a day trip away from the Tennessee River to the south, Reelfoot Lake to the west, and Norris Dam to the east.

There's nothing Margaret loves more than telling natives something they didn't know about their home state. And with 75,000 miles on her station wagon already, she has lots of ideas for little-known places to listen to music, eat barbecue, paddle a lake, hike to a waterfall, or buy works by local artists.

Margaret's work has appeared in national and regional magazines, including *Wine Enthusiast*, *Entrepreneur*, *The Tennessean*, and many others. She is the author of several guidebooks as well as the Nashville Essential Guide, an iPhone app.

Margaret has loved lots of places she's lived, but the day she looked down and realized she was wearing cowboy boots in synagogue, she knew she had become a Tennessean.

19c 3/19 4/19

CPSIA information can be obtained at www.ICGtesting.com
Printed in the USA
LVOW07s0850041115

461068LV00005B/16/P

9 781612 381527